*Traditional Attitudes
and Modern Styles
in Political Leadership*

Seminar papers given at The 28 International Congress of Orientalists will be presented in a series of eight volumes, of which this is the first. The series is edited by Professor A. R. Davis and Dr. Bonnie S. McDougall of the Department of Oriental Studies, The University of Sydney. Other volumes to be published during 1973 and 1974 will deal with the following topics of general relevance to modern Asian societies: irrigation civilizations (convenor J. A. Thompson); the traditional city and modern technology (convenor O. H. K. Spate); the diffusion of material culture (convenor H. H. E. Loofs); the role of law in society (convenor William E. Holder); modern literature and the creative arts (convenor A. R. Davis); music (convenor Willem Adriaansz); Japan in Asia 1930-45 (convenor William H. Newell).

As with previous Congresses, the formal proceedings and abstracts of papers presented will be published in a separate volume.

Traditional Attitudes and Modern Styles in Political Leadership

PAPERS PRESENTED TO
THE 28 INTERNATIONAL CONGRESS
OF ORIENTALISTS UNDER THE
CONVENORSHIP OF J. D. LEGGE

Angus and Robertson · *Publishers*

First published in 1973 by
ANGUS AND ROBERTSON (PUBLISHERS) PTY LTD
102 Glover Street, Cremorne, Sydney
2 Fisher Street, London
159 Block 2, Boon Keng Road, Singapore
P.O. Box 1072, Makati MCC, Rizal, Philippines
107 Elizabeth Street, Melbourne
222 East Terrace, Adelaide
167 Queen Street, Brisbane

National Library of Australia card number
and ISBN 0 207 12710 7

PRINTED IN AUSTRALIA BY WATSON FERGUSON AND CO., BRISBANE

PROCEEDINGS OF THE
28 INTERNATIONAL
CONGRESS
OF ORIENTALISTS
CANBERRA

January 1971

EDITED BY A. R. DAVIS

ASSISTANT EDITOR: BONNIE S. MCDOUGALL

Contents

Foreword

THE FOLLOWING PAPERS were prepared for presentation to a seminar of the 28 International Congress of Orientalists, held in Canberra between 6 and 12 January 1971. In inviting individual scholars to participate no attempt was made to shape contributions according to a closely-defined plan. Rather each contributor was left free, within very broad limits, to bring his or her own expertise to bear upon the general problems of political leadership in Asia and its traditional and modern elements. Nevertheless, the papers as they were eventually presented do show a certain unity of theme.

S. N. Eisenstadt, in his opening paper to the seminar, pointed to the danger of seeing the breakdown of traditional socio-political orders in terms of a European model of transition from tradition to modernity. In fact, the post-traditional orders which emerge in non-European societies, even if they develop supposedly "modern" institutional features, are likely to differ greatly from each other and from the European pattern. As one example, while the European tradition conceives of an anti-thesis between political and social order, traditional societies outside Europe may tend to envisage a coalescence of different functions within the same institution. This sort of difference must affect the kind of post-traditional society likely to emerge. The study of emergent post-traditional orders, Eisenstadt argues, must start from the differing character of various non-European traditions, and the differing ways in which modernity has impinged upon them. His abstract formulations of the problem received concrete embodiment in the empirical studies which followed and which drew attention, in turn, to the possibility of a subtle blend of tradition and modernity within the one individual leader, to the presence of traditional and modern leaderships within the one society, and to the effects of different traditions in shaping the transformation of different societies.

A. R. and D. Willner point, first of all, to the role of charismatic leaders in re-invigorating tradition as part of their attempt to lead their respective societies to modernity. Professor Heesterman contrasts two leaderships in India—the traditional, local leadership of the "little community" and the modern urban leadership of a new intelligentsia—and he argues that political modernization, as borne through British rule, had a limited impact on both. It did not erode the traditional local leadership and it therefore left the new leaders without effective lines of communication to the rural masses. This was a consequence of the nature of modernity itself. "Modernity and traditional order do not lie on the same even line, but on two essentially different planes." Modernization "is not a matter of the modern order pushing out the traditional order", but of an enduring relationship between the two. Modernity in fact "is structurally unable to overthrow the particularism of the little community". Colonial rule thus left no social basis for a national polity in India; and political modernization in the future must depend on a yet-to-be-worked-out relationship between the particularistic order of traditional society and the universalistic order of the nation.

Bernhard Dahm is concerned with contrasts of a not altogether different type. He argues that, while the new élites of Java, Burma and Vietnam resemble each other closely, the differences between the traditional orders of Java and Burma on the one hand (each possessing, he believes, a similar messianic strain) and of Vietnam on the other, have produced a markedly different mass response to an essentially similar impact of colonial rule.

Finally, in a concluding theoretical paper, J. R. Gusfield emphasizes the reflexive character of the notion of tradition, whereby the perception of a traditional culture is a part of a group's self-identification. Members of such a group are to be seen simultaneously as observing or discovering their tradition and as defining it—and thereby in some degree creating it. Their traditional culture is a "belief and a statement about what is *now* perceived as having been typical in the past." The notion that tradition is likely to be, at least in part, a modern manufacture, sits easily enough with the examples discussed by the Willners, Heesterman and Dahm.

However, despite this continuity of theme, the five papers are individual and self-contained essays, tackling problems defined by their respective authors and displaying their own distinctive approaches, and their own special insights: the lightness of touch by which the Willners consider the uses of ethnic humour as an indicator of a developing sense of national identity, for example, or Heesterman's illuminating account of British administration as a loose "husk" covering rather than eroding the little community or his estimate of Gandhi as the authentic renouncer and in consequence the consensus maker for modern India, or Dahm's observations on Buddhism and political action.

*　　*

Scholars of distinction are notoriously individualistic and the bringing together of a panel such as this at an international conference strikes the convener in retrospect as a hazardous enterprise. In fact, however, it did not work out that way. He met with willing co-operation from all, in the pre-Congress correspondence, in the Seminar itself, and in the protracted process of preparing papers for publication. He would like to take this opportunity of expressing his thanks to all of them.

Monash University,
Melbourne, Australia.   J. D. LEGGE

I

Varieties of Post-traditional Social and Political Orders

S. N. EISENSTADT*

I

THE MAJOR PREMISE of this paper is that while we witness throughout the world today a breakdown of traditional socio-political orders, this does not necessarily mean that the development system or order will be patterned according to the initial modern model that developed in Europe, and in fact there may arise a great variety of post-traditional orders. At the same time, they may vary greatly with regard to many other crucial aspects, for example, their very conception of modernity or post-traditionality, as well as their attitude to change and their ability for centre-formation.

In the following paper we shall first briefly analyse the difference between traditional and post-traditional orders. Secondly, we shall point out some of the basic differences between various post-traditional social orders, and finally draw attention to some of the conditions which give rise to them.

II

Within the socio-political order the distinction between a traditional and a modern political or cultural order does not lie in the development, within any institutional sphere, of the

* Professor of Sociology, The Hebrew University of Jerusalem, Israel.

specific structural characteristics which have been often identified as modern—be it the industrial labour force and free markets in the economic sphere, or a centralized administration and unified legal system in the political sphere. Rather it may be seen through the extent to which the basic symbolic and cultural premises of traditionalism, with their structural and cultural limitations, are or are not maintained on the central levels of the societal and cultural orders.

The most important of these premises in the political field are the continuing symbolic and cultural differentiation between the centre and periphery, and the concomitant limitation on the access of members of broader groups to the political centre or centres and their participation within them.

In traditional régimes these premises were closely connected first, to the fact that the legitimation of the rulers was couched in basically traditional religious terms, and second, to the lack of distinction of the basic political role of the subject societal roles, such as, for instance, membership in local communities; and although such membership was often embedded in such groups, the citizens or subjects did not exercise any actual direct or symbolic political rights through a system of voting or franchise.

In the cultural sphere, the basic premises of traditionality, common to all "traditional" societies, however great the differences between them, have been the acceptance of tradition —of the givenness of some past event, order or figure (whether real or symbolic) as the major focus of the collective identity— as the scope and nature of the social and cultural order, the ultimate legitimizer of change, and the delineator of the limits of innovation.

The most important structural derivations of these premises were (a) limitation in terms of reference to some past event of the scope, content and degrees of changes and innovations; (b) limitation of access to positions, the incumbents of which are the legitimate interpreters of the scope and contents of traditions; and (c) limitation of the right to participate in these centres and in forging the legitimate contents and symbols of the social and cultural orders.

Whatever the extent to which the various traditional forms

of life persist in various spheres of society, it is in the changes that have taken place in the connotation of tradition at the central levels that we witness the breakthrough—which may be gradual or abrupt—to some sort of modern socio-political or cultural order. And, in so far as such changes in the connotation of tradition on central levels have not taken place, whatever the extent of structural changes or possible transformation of tradition in different parts of the society, we still have before us some type of traditional order.

Thus, the breakthrough to modernity is focused both in the change in the contents of the symbols of the centre, in their secularization and in the growing emphasis on values of human dignity and social equality as well as in the growing possibility of the participation, even if in an intermittent or partial way, of broader groups in the formulation of its central symbols and institutions.

It is such changes in the connotation of tradition and of their major structural implications that provide the impetus to a continuous process of change and to the perception of change as a positive value in itself, and which create the problem of the absorption of change as the major challenge of modernization.

The preceding analysis brings out perhaps the most central characteristics and problems of modern post-traditional societies—their basic mass-consensual orientation and their predisposition to continuous change.

The consensual or mass aspect of these societies is rooted in the growing impingement of broader strata on the centre, in their demands to participate in the sacred symbols of society and in their formulation, and in the replacement of the traditional symbols by new ones which stress these participatory and social dimensions.

This tendency to broad mass-consensuality does not, of course, find its fullest institutionalized expression in all types of modern societies. In many régimes in the first stages of modernization it may be weak or intermittent, while totalitarian régimes naturally tend to suppress its fullest expression. But even totalitarian régimes attempt to legitimize themselves in terms of such values and it is impossible to understand their policies and their attempts to create symbols of mass-consensus without taking into consideration their assumption of the existence of such a consensual tendency among its strata and the acknowledgement of its existence by the rulers.

III

The preceding discussion brings out some of the most salient characteristics and problems in modern political orders. First, it brings out the fact that it is the breakthrough from a traditional socio-political order in the direction of a mass-consensual one that contains within itself the specific characteristics of social changes in modernity: the propensity to system-transformation and the persistence of. demands of change, protest and transformation. These demands for change could, of course, develop in different directions; they could be reformatory, demanding the improvement of existing institutions or they could aim at the total transformation of a system.

Second, it indicates that modernization evinces two closely connected, yet distinct aspects. The first is the development of a social structure with a great variety of structural differentiation and diversification, of continuously changing structural forms, activities and problems and propensities to continuous change and system transformation. But the mere development of these propensities does not in itself assume the development of an institutional structure which is capable of dealing in a relatively stable way with these continuous changes and concomitantly assuring the maintenance of a civil order.

Thus, the crucial problem that modernization creates in its wake is that of the ability of the emerging social structure to deal with such continuous changes or, in other words, the problem of sustained development, i.e., the ability to develop an institutional structure which is capable of "absorbing" continuously changing problems and demands. It is this which constitutes the central challenge and subsequent problem of modernization. This is the challenge of modernity, and of post-traditional social orders.

IV

Such a breakthrough to a non-traditional socio-political order necessarily poses before the respective society the problem of defining in some new ways the scope and nature of the socio-cultural orders and of their collective identity, and of re-organizing in a new form the perception of the major para-meters of the cultural and social orders.

The first such breakthrough from a traditional to a modern social order took place in Europe and it was here that the problem of defining such an order in new terms became first fully articulated. The first definition of the parameters of the modern social order has therefore been closely related to the specific characteristics of the symbolic institutional pattern of the modern socio-political order that has developed in the West and constituted, in a sense, part of this pattern or universe.

The major form of this socio-political order—in the post-Counter-Reformation period, throughout the eighteenth and nineteenth centuries, and later in the United States, Australia, Canada etc.—was the nation-state. The major characteristics of this type of modern socio-political order have been enumera-ted as (a) a high degree of congruence between the cultural and the political identities of the territorial population; (b) a high level of symbolic and effective commitments to the centre and a close relation between these centres and the more primordial dimensions of human existence; and (c) a marked emphasis on common politically-defined collective goals for all members of the national community.

In greater detail, this model assumed that all the major com-ponents of centre-formation—i.e., first, the institutionalization, both in symbolic and organizational terms, of the quest for some charismatic ordering of social and cultural experience, and for some participation in such orders; second, the crystal-lization of the common societal and cultural collective identity based on common attributes or on participation in common symbolic events; third, the crystallization and articulation of collective goals; fourth, the regulation of intrasocietal and intergroup relations; and fifth, the regulation of internal and external power-relations—tend to converge around the political centre of the nation-state.

In many ways, many of these characteristics of the European nation-state were derived or transmitted from several parts of their pre-modern socio-political traditions, that is, from imperial traditions, and from those of city-states and feudal societies. They combined the strong activist orientation of the city-state, the broad conception, to be found in many imperial traditions, of the political order as actively related to the cosmic or cultural order, and finally the tradition of the great religions and the pluralistic elements of feudalism.

In the European (especially Western European) tradition these various orientations were rooted in a social structure characterized by a relatively high degree of commitment of various groups and strata to the cultural and political orders and their centres, as well as by a high degree of autonomy in their access to these orders and their respective centres.

It was out of these orientations that some of the specific assumptions about the patterns of participation and about the protest characteristics of the nation-state developed. The most important of these assumptions was that the political forces, the political élites and the more autonomous social forms—the state on the one hand and "society" on the other—continuously struggle over their relative importance in the formation and crystallization of the cultural and political centre of the nation-state and in the regulation of access to it; that the various processes of structural change and dislocation—which the periphery was continuously undergoing as a result of the processes of modernization—give rise not only to various concrete problems and demands, but also to a growing quest for participation in the broader social and political order; and that this quest of the periphery for participation in such social, political and cultural orders is primarily manifested in the search for access to these centres.

V

The background of most non-European traditional societies differed greatly from that of Europe, and so, in consequence, did the post-traditional orders that developed within them.

In many, especially tribal societies the existence of centres or relatively homogeneous ethnic or national communities could not be taken for granted. Even in societies—like the imperial or patrimonial ones—in which there could be no doubt about the existence of a specific centre and state-apparatus, the very interrelations of the state, of the political order, with the social order have been envisaged in ways different from those of the Western tradition.

In general most of these societies did not share the imperial, city-state and feudal traditions which were specific to the European traditional order. Thus, for instance, in the imperial Asian societies—as in Russia or Japan—the pluralistic elements were much weaker than in feudal society or in city-states. In Russia, for example, there was no conception of a relatively autonomous access of the major strata to the political and cultural centres and the cultural orders were often perceived as subservient to the political one. Similarly, in Japan, there existed a conception of the close identity between the cosmic and political order and a very high degree of the unconditional commitment of broader strata to the centre which represented this cosmic-political identity. In many other societies—in Southeast Asia, in Africa, and to some degree in Latin America—the forces of (later) modernity impinged on patrimonial systems where the level of commitment to a socio-political order was much smaller, and in which also the active, autonomous relation between the political and the cosmic order was much weaker, even if there existed a closer coalescence between the two.

Their political traditions envisaged but rarely the sort of split or dichotomy between state and society which was to be found within the European tradition. Instead, they tended more to stress the congruent but often passive relations between the cosmic order on the one hand and the socio-political order on the other. Unlike the Western tradition, the interrelation between the political and the social orders was not envisaged in terms of an antithesis between two entities or powers; rather, it was more often stated in terms of the coalescence of different functions within the same group or organization, centred around a common focus in the cosmic order.

As a result of these differences—as well as of differences in the impingement of the forces of modernity and their respective experiences of modernization—there developed different types of post-traditional social and political orders.

VI

But beyond these differences between weak and strong centres, the study of new nations opens up before us the possibility of various contents of modern centres. The various differences in political organization and participation in many of the new nations may indicate not only differences in the strength of the centre in terms of the people's present or future commitment to it, but also of different types of contents of the different centres—the political, cultural and societal centres—and of their interrelationship. In many of these countries we find a lesser symbolic autonomy of the specific cultural and/or political centre, and a much greater degree of segregation between these different types of centres, each of which may also encompass a different geographical locus.

These differences in content may be very closely connected with the development of different patterns of political ideology, with various conceptions of the political and the cosmic cultural orders, and of relations between the technical, administrative and symbolic aspects of political order and the behaviour of rulers, which differ greatly from those which have developed in the framework of the European tradition.

These necessarily give rise to different patterns of collective identity and of political participation and struggle from those which developed in the European or other post-imperial centres. They may also give rise to régimes in which there is a much smaller identity between political and cultural centres, i.e., in which the "nation-state" no longer constitutes the "natural" unit of a modern political order.

These differences could already have been discerned from the beginning of the spread of modernization beyond Western Europe to Russia and Japan, where there developed new patterns of such orders, which with the further spread of modernity served as models, and to which we shall briefly refer below. But these differences can be most clearly seen in the shaping of post-traditional socio-political orders in many of the countries which have not adopted any of these models—especially in the various countries of Latin America, Southeast Asia and Africa. The centres were characterized by what may be called "modern" patrimonialism, i.e., the establishment or continuation of new political and administrative central frameworks which have a tendency to maintain the external contents of traditional or modern symbols without simultaneously maintaining any strong commitments to them. Such centres have tended to display almost exclusive concern for the preservation of the existing weak frameworks of power, thus giving rise to a continuous succession of weak centres.

The major difference between these régimes and seemingly similar régimes that developed frameworks of strong centres was in their low ability effectively to mobilize new political forces, and to create viable modern institutional frameworks capable of dealing with problems of absorption of change.

VII

These differences tended to manifest themselves both in the types of political organizations and in the nature of the crises specific to such types of régimes. In almost all these cases there initially tended to develop some very weak modern centres.

Perhaps the best illustrations of such differences can be seen in the functions of parties, of voting and of political participation. All of these tend to develop in all types of modern centres, and yet with wide differences among them so far as their significance in the political process is concerned.

A few illustrations may help to make this point clear. First, it can be seen that the function of parties seems to vary greatly among them. The tendency to monolithic, and yet not totalitarian parties, or to single, non-totalitarian party régimes in many new states suggests that many of these parties should be seen more as instruments for the forging of some new common collective identities than as instruments for the struggle between different contestants for power, representing different interests and/or ideological orientations. The latter struggles seem to take place inside such parties rather than between them.

Concurrently, bureaucracies may be often seen not only as administrative branches of the centre or as small groups or cliques contending for power within it, but also as custodians of whatever common symbols may exist; and indeed they may represent whatever civil order can be maintained. As a result, they may compete with the parties for the full representation of the centre, a fact which can perhaps to some degree explain the quick succession of a party régime by a military régime, yet with each régime maintaining some of the organizational framework and activities of its predecessor.

The differences between strong and weak centres can be seen in the nature, and especially in the outcome, of crises and breakdowns that may occur within them. The general reasons and symptoms of such crises and breakdowns, the rifts and cleavages between different types of élites, between the central and the parochial symbols and identities, between precontractual and contractual symbols and between classes and regions, are to a large extent common to all of them. But the nature both of the crises and of their outcomes tends to differ.

In régimes with strong centres, crises usually tend to focus around problems of integrating new groups within such centres. In societies with weak centres the situation is very different. The specific crises or problems with which the latter régimes are faced are, first, their effectiveness on the new modern international scene, and, second, the upsurge of unregulated demands of various broader groups which are very often fostered and catered for by these élites, with the resulting waste of resources. They are confronted with potentially continuous conflicts within the élite and the new centres. The crises and problems that may develop out of the great intensity of the conflicts between traditionalistic and more modern élites, the new modern ways in which the claims of many of these groups are being made and the contradictory assumptions of these groups about the nature of the centre itself and the bases of its legitimation, may minimize the possibilities of establishing new, stable and viable centres of any kind.

Similarly, the outcomes seem to differ. In societies with strong centres the tendency is more a "total", dramatic breakdown of the centre, possibly leading to its reconstitution on a new level. In societies with weaker centres, such instability and oscillation often tend to continue with mobilization, partial economic development and political activity. They may lead to a continuous succession of weak, patrimonial centres, together with economic regression and growing political apathy.

But these régimes also tend to vary greatly with regard to such dimensions as the scope of political mobilization, the relative predominance of different institutional settings (bureaucracy, military, political parties), the relations between political and ethnic-national communities or the degree of relative stability of their respective régimes and collective political and cultural boundaries, and their respective ability to deal with the changes arising out of the encounter of the centres established by them with the new, continuously-changing social forces.

Last, and of great importance, is the structure of the international setting in which the process of modernization takes place, the distribution of political and economic power among the various societies and strata, and the types and processes of dominance and dependence that tend to develop among them.

It is the interaction among these various variables subsumed under the three broad conditions mentioned briefly above—the different socio-political directions and traditions of these societies in their pre-modern settings, the nature of the impingement of modernization on them, and the structure of the situation of change—that can, it seems to us, explain the development of different patterns of post-traditional socio-political orders, and the changes of any one society from one pattern to another.

VIII

A focal point around which these various conditions converge is the nature of the different types of élites, and their centre-formation and institution-building capacities.

In the creation of these élites, of special importance is the interrelation among degrees of solidarity of different groups and strata, structural and symbolic autonomy of different social spheres (i.e., the degree of rigidity or flexibility of these spheres), the strength or weakness of the major centres of the symbolic orders (i.e., the social, political and cultural, and usually in the case of traditional societies, religious centres), that can best—even if in a limited and preliminary way—explain the development within a given society of élites and groups with different degrees of organizational, innovative and transformative capacities. These tend to compete strongly among themselves for relative predominance in the emerging social structure. It would be impossible to go into all the possible variations—we shall present here only some general hypotheses. Further research would be necessary to enable us to go beyond these very rough generalizations.

First, it seems that in a society, or parts thereof, characterized by relatively high solidarity but low flexibility, relatively traditionalistic but well-organized groups will tend to develop. On the other hand, in a society, or parts thereof, which is characterized by a high level of flexibility but a relatively low level of solidarity, there may develop several relatively adaptable but not very well-organized groups or strata. When in such a society there also exists a high level of solidarity, then we might expect the development of relatively well-organized and adaptable groups or élites.

But the extent to which élite groups are able to influence their broader institutional settings, and especially the more central institutional cores of the society, will primarily depend on the types of centres which exist within their societies and their relation to these centres. The capacity to affect the broader institutional settings will be smaller among élites which are relatively non-cohesive, which are alienated from other élites and from the broader groups and strata of the society, and which are either very distant from the existing centre and/or succeed in totally monopolizing it to the exclusion of other groups and élites. In terms of centre-building most such groups will tend to emphasize the maintenance of some given attributes of collective identity together with the regulation of internal and external force.

In those societies, or parts thereof, in which there exists a high level of rigidity in the social system and its symbolic orders —i.e., where there is relatively little symbolic distinction between the different social and cultural orders, together with relatively weak centres, as seems to have been the case in many Southeast Asian patrimonial régimes—there will tend to develop relatively traditionalistic, non-transformative élites which still may evince a certain organizational capacity and some predisposition for limited technical innovation.

Side by side with such élites there may also under such conditions develop, especially within the less cohesive sectors of the societies, various new ideological, professional or political groups, with some positive orientations to change, but with relatively small transformative capacities beyond the adaptation of new ideologies or symbols and with little ability for continuous institutional activity.

Both types of élites which develop in such conditions will tend to develop "closeness" in their social and status perception and a ritual emphasis on certain specific and very limited types of status orientations. They will conceive their own legitimation in terms of maintaining these restricted ranges of status symbols.

Most élites which develop in such conditions, in so far as they attempt to be active in centre-formation, tend to emphasize one of the components of centre-building—especially the maintenance of symbols of common identity or the regulation of external and internal forces—but they usually tend less to stress the other components, especially the regulation of centre-group relations and the development of *new* goals and symbols of common identity.

In so far as such conditions of rigidity of the social and cultural order and the concomitant resistance to change coexist with a rather strong centre, there might also develop from within some sectors—probably from within those groups not too distant from the centre and enjoying some internal solidarity—militant élites with strong innovative, albeit coercive orientations.

The more centre-oriented of such élites tend in their centre-building activities to stress the *combination* of the development of common identity and force as well as the development of new collective goals, with a small degree of non-coercive regulation of intergroup relations.

The existence within societies, or sectors thereof, of a great degree of structural and cultural autonomy and flexibility, especially when connected with the existence of high cohesion of social groups, may facilitate the development of élites with a relatively high level of adaptability to change, but not necessarily with great transformative capacities.

Here also it is the symbolic and institutional structure of the centres—their strength or weakness—which is of crucial importance to the extent to which there may develop more transformative élites. In so far as there exist such conditions of flexibility, together with strong and almost by definition open centres, it seems that the possibility of the development of highly transformative élites is greater.

Under such conditions, as research on inactive élites within various micro- and macro-societal settings indicates, such transformative capacities are mostly to be found among élites which are relatively cohesive, with a strong sense of self-identity. This is true especially among secondary élites which, while somewhat distant from the central ruling one, either maintain positive solidary orientations to the centre and are not entirely alienated from the pre-existing élites and from some of the broader groups of the society, or manage to function within relatively segregated institutional spheres.

Such élites also tend to develop simultaneous orientations to collective ideological transformation and to concrete tasks and problems in different "practical" fields and they perceive their own legitimation in terms of such wider changes and not only in terms of providing various immediate benefits or status symbols to other groups.

It is such élites which tend, from the point of view of centre-building, to assure the larger degree of flexibility in terms of combining various components of the centre. They especially tend to emphasize the combination of a relatively non-coercive regulation of intergroup relations, together with the creation of new symbols of common identity and possibly the development of new types of collective goals.

In so far as in conditions of relatively high flexibility of the social structure there exist relatively weak centres, the development of such transformative élites is usually greatly impeded. Instead there may develop a great variety of both traditionalistic and highly adaptable élites, each with different orientations. In so far as no balance of power develops among them, the very development of such multiplicity may jeopardize the successful institutionalization of a new viable institutional structure.

The centres that may be built by these élites may then be characterized by a high level of coalition-building ability but also by a much smaller ability to develop binding common attributes of identity or to crystallize collective goals.

IX

The preceding analysis of the conditions of development of different types of élites and their centre-building activities may seem to have been put in a rather deterministic way. This was not our intention. As has been pointed out above, in every complex society there always exist rather heterogeneous conditions and a variety of sectors, each of which may produce different kinds of élites. Among such élites there usually develops a strong competition as to their relative predominance, and the emerging situation which results from such competition is never fully predetermined.

The relative lack of predetermination is emphasized even more if we bear in mind the importance of the international setting and its relation to the development of various élites.

Throughout our discussion we have stressed the crucial importance of various secondary élites or movements as potential bearers of socio-political transformation. But the structural locations of these élites seem to differ greatly among the various types of political régimes, mainly according to the nature of the division of labour prevalent within a society on the one hand, and the relative placement of these élites within the internal system of the societies or within the international settings of their respective societies on the other.

In general, it seems that in so far as the division of labour within any given social system is either "mechanical" and/or based on a centre which is focused primarily on regulation of force and/or on the upholding of symbols of common identity, then the probability is that change-oriented or transformative cultural or political élites would develop mainly within the international enclaves around the society and less *within* these societies. However, the probability of its effecting change in the societies would depend on the breakdown of the centre because of some external or internal forces and/or by finding some secondary internal groups or élites which for either ideological or interest factors would become its allies.

On the other hand, in so far as a social system is characterized by a high degree of organic solidarity, and/or within its centre there is an emphasis on the combination of all components of centre-building, and especially on the regulation of intergroup relations and common symbols of identity, the probability would be that a change-oriented élite would develop, to some extent at least, from within the society, although it would also be closely related to broader international settings and enclaves.

The probability of its becoming effective would then depend more on the interrelations between it and existing centres on the one hand, and the broader groups on the other—interrelations which have been briefly discussed above.

II

Charismatic Political Leadership as Conservator and Catalyst

ANN RUTH WILLNER and DOROTHY WILLNER*

T HIS PAPER deals with three notions concerning charismatic political leadership and with some relationships that may be implied by and perceived among them. The first notion, suggested by the cases of Sukarno and U Nu, is that of the charismatic political leader as conservator of tradition. The second is that of the commonly-held image of the charismatic leader as the catalyst of change, particularly with respect to ex-colonial states. The third is the notion of the charismatic leader as revolutionary, derived from the classic Weberian formulation.

We have elsewhere indicated two kinds of connections between tradition and charismatic leadership. The generation of a charismatic relationship between a leader and his followers, we stated, is in large part dependent upon the leader's ability to draw upon and manipulate the traditional myths and symbols of his culture.[1] Furthermore, in seeking to create

* Respectively Professor of Political Science and Professor of Anthropology, The University of Kansas, U.S.A.

[1] Ann Ruth Willner and Dorothy Willner, "The Rise and Role of Charismatic Leaders", *Annals of the American Academy of Political and Social Science*, CCCLIV (March 1965), pp. 82-84.

cohesion, charismatic leaders in new states utilized tradition, attempting to link traditional symbols and values to innovation.[2] Here we should like to pursue this theme further and suggest that, in so doing, they tend to conserve and even to reinvigorate some aspects of the traditional heritage.

This line of thought would seem on the surface to be at odds with Max Weber's treatment of charisma as repudiating the past and "in this sense a specifically revolutionary force".[3] However, this apparent contradiction disappears if we clarify which past is being referred to. It is likely that Weber thought in terms of a previous or existing social and political order in a state with a continuous history. The phenomenon of charismatic leadership as a force against colonialism in areas with sharply discontinuous histories was not striking in Weber's time. If the "past" is equated with the colonial order, then charismatic leaders in what became new states did indeed repudiate it. But their vision of the desired new order to come did incorporate elements of the pre-colonial past, as exemplified by Gandhi's affirmation of Hindu ethos and many practices and his celebration of the virtues of traditional village life,[4] by U Nu's emphasis on the Aśokan Buddhist tradition,[5] and by Sukarno's stress on gotong-royong, the traditional village mode of mutual assistance.[6]

Neither Weber nor many of those who have followed him in equating charismatic with revolutionary leadership[7] have been precise in their use of the term "revolutionary". Leaders have

[2]*Ibid.*, pp. 86-87.

[3]Max Weber, *The Theory of Social and Economic Organization*, ed. by Talcott Parsons (Oxford University Press, New York, 1947), p. 362.

[4]For an excellent study of Gandhi as a charismatic leader, see Lloyd I. Rudolph and Susanne Hoeber Rudolph, *The Modernity of Tradition: Political Development in India* (University of Chicago Press, Chicago, 1967).

[5]See Emanuel Sarkisyanz, *Buddhist Backgrounds of the Burmese Revolution* (Nijhoff, The Hague, 1965); also Richard A. Butwell, *U Nu of Burma* (Stanford University Press, Stanford, 1963).

[6]For a detailed study of some of these practices, see Koentjaraningraat, *Some Social-Anthropological Observations on Gotong Rojong Practices in Two Villages of Central Java* (Cornell University Press, Ithaca, 1961).

[7]For distinctions between these two categories, see Ann Ruth Willner, *Charismatic Political Leadership: A Theory* (Princeton University, Center of International Studies, Princeton, 1968), pp. 10-13.

been labelled as "revolutionary" according to any of the following criteria: (1) the espousal of revolutionary goals; (2) the seizure of power by revolutionary means or as a consequence of conditions of revolution; (3) the revolutionary transformation of a society. Many, although not all, modern charismatic leaders can satisfy the first criterion; some, indeed, gained much of their charismatic appeal from proclaiming revolutionary objectives. Fewer can be seen as revolutionary according to the second criterion.[8] Even fewer satisfy the third criterion, that of performance. In a strictly political sense, the replacement of colonial bureaucratic rule by a national government, the founding fathers of some new states might qualify as revolutionary. But if revolutionary transformation is taken to refer to fundamental changes in the social order, very few contemporary charismatic leaders qualify. In Asia, Mao and Ho Chi Minh would, but not U Nu or Sukarno; in the Western hemisphere, Castro, but neither Franklin D. Roosevelt nor Juan Peron.

If charismatic leaders have not, by and large, effected revolutionary changes in the societies they led, what changes have they effected? It is generally recognized that they have catalyzed various processes often subsumed under the term "nation-building". They have done so, at least in part, by bringing to the fore traditional myths, symbols and customs, many of which had become attenuated. In invoking tradition, whether as a means of generating national pride or as a vehicle for the communication of unfamiliar ideas,[9] they re-invigorated it.

As they re-enacted on the contemporary stage, by their styles of life and modes of self-presentation, the historical and legendary dramas of just and benevolent rulers, saintly ascetics and magically-endowed empire-builders,[10] they revitalized

---

[8]Peron would meet this criterion whereas Hitler and Mussolini would not, having gained formal power by the normal processes of their polity.

[9]See Sarkisyanz, *op. cit.* and Rudolph & Rudolph, *op. cit.* for illustrations of the ways in which U Nu and Gandhi communicated modern ideas in the traditional idiom of Buddhism and Hinduism respectively.

[10]The references are respectively to U Nu's association with Setkya Min and Mindon Min, to Gandhi, and to Sukarno's having been seen as Kĕrtanāgara.

these images and the values associated with them. In Indonesia, for example, supporters of the current régime might not have felt it necessary to disseminate rumours about President Suharto's possession of magical krisses and similar sacred relics, had Sukarno not given new life to the association of these with a leader's power. The attempts to infuse the doctrine of *Pancasila* with new content, the creation of new symbols and acronyms for new cabinets and endeavours and other traditional practices testify to Sukarno's strengthening of tradition. Similarly, the attempts by the Ne Win régime to utilize the traditional folk festival, the *pwé*, as a peasant seminar may be traced to U Nu's elevation of folk tradition.[11]

Not all leaders strove, as did Sukarno, to give national institutions a traditional cast by elevating customary modes of behaviour in local communities into national decision-making procedures. But even what from one perspective might be considered a modernizing change in the conduct of political life, i.e. the extensive travel of these leaders and their direct contact with thousands upon thousands of people, may be seen from another vantage point as restoring an element of tradition. When contrasted with the impersonal and remote rule by law and edict of colonialism, the visibility and accessibility of these leaders revived the image of the benevolent ruler who personally cared about his subjects and their welfare.

II

The term "nation-building" refers to many processes for which charismatic leaders have served as catalyst. These processes involve the development of nation-wide institutions and the development of a national identity. The activities and successes of charismatic leaders in promoting educational activities and building political organizations, as well as in mobilizing vast segments of their populations into the political arena, need not be dwelt on here. Our concern is rather with the development of national identities.

National identity can be seen as encompassing at least three analytically distinct, although empirically overlapping and

[11]John H. Badgley, "Two Styles of Military Rule: Thailand and Burma", *Government and Opposition*, IV (1969), p. 106.

interrelated dimensions. The first of these is that of personal identification with the nation, i.e. the individual's perception of and commitment to membership in the collectivity constituting a national state. Of the other two dimensions, one may be termed "horizontal integration", referring to the integrative aspects of national identity in transcending local and parochial loyalties; the other can be called "vertical integration", i.e. national identity as a bridge to span the famous "gap" between educated urban élites and the rural masses.

Since charismatic leaders have engaged in a variety of activities which would seem to contribute to the development of national identities, it seems plausible to infer and assert, as has so often been inferred and asserted, that they have done so. However, such assertions can be treated with scepticism in the absence of evidence that their activities have met with success and in the absence of criteria for specifying an increase in national identity. Therefore, rather than merely assert that Sukarno catalyzed the development of Indonesian national identity, we will offer some evidence for this and, at the same time, suggest indicators that may prove useful for assessing the growth of national identities.

Personal observations of differences in behaviour in similar contexts of action in Indonesia between the early 1950s and the late 1960s suggest that some of the earlier problems of identity would appear to have been resolved. At minimum, they can be lived with and coped with in ways that do not impinge on and critically affect other arenas of decision and action. Some of the indicators found relevant in arriving at this conclusion relate to (1) the uses of language, (2) the uses of humour and related sensitivity to criticism, (3) the transformation of parochial symbols into national ones and (4) the conscious concern with equality.

It is almost redundant to note that problems of personal identity in relation to national identity were problems for the indigenous élites of new states, not for their village-based masses.[12] It was the Westernized and partly-Westernized

---

[12]For a study of this in Burma, see Lucian W. Pye, *Politics, Personality and Nation Building: Burma's Search for Identity* (Yale University Press, New Haven, 1962).

élites who suffered the sense of insecurity and uncertainty engendered by the colonial experience. Both in communication among themselves and with foreigners, this could be seen in problems connected with language in the early 1950s. Members of the Indonesian political élite spoke at least three languages, that of their own ethnic groups, Dutch and Indonesian. But ease of communication might be one of the least important of the factors that entered into the decision of which language to use among themselves, when and with whom. Thus, an Indonesian of Javanese ethnic background might be involved in the dilemma of trying to decide whether he would be seen as too traditional if he used Javanese or if he did not, as denying his ethnic background; too Dutch-minded if he used Dutch or conversely, insufficiently nationalistic; too poorly educated if he used Indonesian or too aggressively nationalist. Now, any of these languages and several additional foreign ones are used alternatively and simultaneously and, most significantly, unselfconsciously, according to the convenience of the parties engaged in communication.

A similar ease can now be detected in encounters between an Indonesian and a foreigner. In the past, even under conditions in which the familiarity of each with the other's language was known, psychological tensions could result as the Indonesian had difficulty in deciding whether to assert his national identity in using his own language or to assert his equality in using the foreigner's, and the foreigner wondered whether he was more likely to flatter or insult the Indonesian by addressing him in Indonesian. The foreign language is still more likely to be the most frequent medium of communication, but only because Indonesians are more multilingual than the foreigners they most frequently encounter. In this context, it might be noted that some of the Indonesians who formerly fought against the use of Dutch in their universities are now urging their children to learn it as an additional language.

Indonesians are noted for their humour and their enjoyment of jokes and puns, many of them not without an element of malice. The real or fancied foibles of one ethnic group have frequently formed the butt of the jokes of another, but jokes told largely within the confines of that group or to fictive kin.

When a Sundanese openly teases a member of the matriarchal Minangkabau with being dominated by his mother-in-law and the Minangkabau man laughs, it is a sign that some of the denominators of ethnic difference have been transcended.

Another indicator reflecting the relative strength or weakness of personal-cum-national identity is the type and quality of reactions to criticisms from extra-national sources. For example, in the past questions or admonitions concerning corruption from Americans provoked silent humiliation in Indonesians or feelings of shame that they and their country did not measure up to modern standards. Now an American might well be told in return that the original benefactor of the foundation funds on which he is now travelling might not have been untainted.

It might be noted that the abovementioned indicators—the uses of humour and related sensitivity to criticism—as well as the following ones, the transformation of parochial symbols into more broadly national symbols and the conscious concern with equality, refer not only to the personal identification dimension of national identity but also to the dimensions of horizontal and vertical integration.

Modernity for Indonesians in the early 1950s was equated with Westernization. Thus, a foreigner who wished to learn something about *dukuns* (folk-healers), *guna-guna* (spells), *pusakas* (magically-endowed sacred relics) or *ludruk* (folk drama) had to resort to servants or villagers, if he could command their language. His friends among the Indonesian élite were of little assistance, having scant knowledge of traditional or folk culture or inhibited about admitting to this knowledge. *Malu*, or shame, at the prospect of being scorned as "primitive" could extend down to the village head who was startled and embarrassed at being asked by a foreigner when his village held its ritual purification ceremony. Before replying, he asked whether the foreigner did not consider such rituals "animistic". At present, a successful Indonesian bureaucrat, entrepreneur or military man might recommend a *dukun* as well as a doctor to his foreign visitor and take him to a *ludruk* performance.

A retired Javanese statesman, equally at home with Aeschylus and Proust, may today deplore his grandchildren's preoccupation with rock-and-roll. But he admits that in his youth he knew little of Indonesian history while able to name every important Dutch general and river, whereas his grandchildren are also studying Javanese *gamelan*. They and their parents are familiar with Teuku Umar, hero of Achenese history and myth, and Achenese also count the Javanese Prince Diponegara among their heroes.

The last-mentioned phenomenon is not restricted to élites and sub-élites. A survey of mass and middle-level strata of the population indicated changes between the early 1950s and the present. Formerly, Indonesians of rural provenience or one generation removed from villages or small towns would identify themselves according to ethnic group, if asked their nationality. Now they are more likely to reply with the term "Indonesian". Formerly, when asked to name or describe national, historical, mythical or contemporary heroes, their answers would be largely restricted to those of their own ethnic areas. Now many answers in this survey included names from the histories and legends of other ethnic areas than their own. Moreover, in assigning values to heroes of the revolutionary period and earlier, some favoured figures from other ethnic areas over those of their own.

Not only increased horizontal integration but increased vertical integration is indicated by the broader sharing of a sense of Indonesian nationality and of a common stock of symbols. The continued sharing of pre-existing elements of a common political culture was evident from this survey as well as from interviews with élite leaders of various political persuasion. Such elements include: (1) the importance of personal qualities of an individual leader, however they may be ascertained, over that of any set of institutional arrangements for providing leadership; (2) a preference for the exercise of leadership in paternalistic but non-authoritarian fashion; (3) the concern with settling disputes by processes which blur and superficially reconcile issues of controversy in the interests of maintaining an often fictitious unity.

A more conscious interest in equality or at least in diminishing the appearances of recognized existing inequalities exists today, when compared with the past, in statements and actions of members of both élite and mass strata. There were indications in the early post-Independence years that for many members of élite groups equality meant little more than equality for them with their former colonial rulers. As one Indonesian worker expressed it, "they talk a great game of democracy, but for me it is *omong-kosong*, empty talk." Yet, an attempt by a high-status Indonesian official to treat his country cousin as a social equal might cause the latter agonies of embarrassment.

Status distinctions at the current time can less easily be detected by such denominators as differences in dress, language and demeanour, even in Java where such distinctions were once so pronounced. Keeping their chauffeurs contented has been a major concern in the daily lives of members of élite strata. In Djakarta, one occasionally sees servants and masters sitting together to watch television programmes.

Perhaps economic hardship, more than Sukarno's strictures and his elevation of symbols of the common man, has served as a leveller of social distance. Women of aristocratic and gentry lineage, whose activities were formerly restricted to their homes, clubs and charities, in recent years began to rival their lower-class sisters in the extent, if not the same type, of entrepreneurial activities. Some of the earlier distinctions between masters and servants were blurred as they jointly began to participate in some form of a partnership basis in the rental of taxis, the production and distribution of home-made products or other economic enterprises, and as they began to bargain on the basis of how the fruits should be shared.

III

Although charismatic leaders of new states in Asia have undeniably catalyzed changes in the countries they have led, these changes, as we have suggested above, cannot really be considered revolutionary transformation. Perhaps the one exception to this argument is the case of Ho Chi Minh. For revolutionary change refers to drastic transformations of the total socio-economic order effected by or resulting from the alteration of the political system. Since revolutionary change, as defined here, leads to the elimination of institutions that formed the basis for the previous social order, that order cannot easily be reconstructed. In this sense, revolutionary change tends to be irreversible.

However, Indonesia under Sukarno and Burma under U Nu underwent traditionalization rather than socio-economic development.[13] Production declined, public institutions decayed and public administration deteriorated. In Indonesia, the state of public highways and incidents of private collecting of tolls from those using them as late as 1968 suggest that the process of traditionalization had not yet been arrested.

The analogy of charismatic leader as catalyst of change may help us understand the failure of such leaders as agents of development. The term "catalyst" is, of course, derived from chemistry where it refers to an agent which not only induces a chemical reaction but itself remains unchanged at the end of the reaction. Pursuing this analogy, we may look not only to the changes catalyzed by charismatic leaders in new states in Asia but to the goals of the leaders themselves and whether these goals changed in the course of the leaders' careers. Initially, their goals included political independence for what had been a colony and a state encompassing at least the same territory as the colony. But did their goals really include economic development and revolutionary transformation of the social order? Sukarno devoted considerable rhetoric to the exploitation of man by man and the need for a social revolution; U Nu spoke frequently of the Welfare State. Sukarno was always a self-stated Marxist, as Dahm has shown.[14] But did Sukarno's conception of Marxism include an explicit programme for the economic and social transformation of his society?

Following up the analogy of catalyst, we suggest that the charismatic leaders of the new states of Asia had limitless but nebulous visions as to the nature of the new society and that

[13]See Ann Ruth Willner, *The Neotraditional Accommodation to Political Independence: The Case of Indonesia* (Princeton University, Center of International Studies, Princeton, 1966) and James F. Guyot, "Political Involution in Burma", *Journal of Comparative Administration*, II, 3 (November 1970), pp. 299-322.

[14]Bernhard Dahm, *Sukarno and the Struggle for Indonesian Independence* (Cornell University Press, Ithaca, 1969).

their specific goals were limited. After Independence they used their charisma to hold the state together and to strengthen bonds of nationhood among its disparate members. But although their post-Independence societies changed as the years passed, the leaders did not. They did not become oriented to development as a primary goal; they did not seek to glorify higher standards of productivity, rational administrative practices, hard work and frugality in the service of the state. Sukarno danced with workers; he did not pin medals on worker-heroes. U Nu donned the saffron robe, not the garb of a farmer in a new co-operative.

It is undoubtedly an oversimplification, although not substantially incorrect, to suggest that these leaders lost charisma for some strategic élites, if not for the masses, because of their neglect of development. As long as holding a state together and building national unity seemed urgent, then they were acceptable as national leaders to those for whom they lacked charismatic appeal and even to their critics and opponents.[15] But when these tasks no longer seemed crucial, the agenda changed even for some supporters of the leaders. Convinced that the time had come to stress economic development and effective administration, these élites could become allies of those who previously had pressed for these goals. For such strategic groups, the seeming unwillingness or inability of their leaders to revise their priorities rendered them obsolete and ultimately disposable.

If charismatic leaders of new states in Asia did not catalyze development because it was not really one of their goals, this could be assimilated to the Weberian ideal-type construction according to which charismatic figures reject rational economic conduct. However, this would not apply to all the charismatic national leaders of recent decades, even in Asia, e.g. Ho and certainly Mao, or, to go outside of Asia, Lenin, Roosevelt, de Gaulle. The fact that China and the U.S.S.R., France and the United States are not new states suggests alternative hypotheses, e.g. (1) that development had been one of the original post-

---

[15]An illustration of this was Sjahrir's discouraging his followers from trying to oust Sukarno while he himself had been interned.

Independence goals of the leaders of new states in Asia but, confronted by the exigencies of nation-building and the inadequacy of the resources at hand, they had deferred such goals; (2) that they had rejected economic development, Western-style, as part of their rejection of colonialism, and were in search of autochthonous styles of development; (3) the related hypothesis that their development goals were socialistic, but that they lacked both the power and the resources to implement socialist modes of development without imposing a coercive dictatorship.

We do not wish, in this paper, to assess the validity of such hypotheses and choose among these or others. Rather let us speculate whether Sukarno and U Nu, given the resources available to them, could have used their charisma to catalyze development in their respective countries, as they seem to have catalyzed or, at least, contributed to nation-building.

Charismatic leaders, as we have seen, draw on, are sustained by, and manipulate myth and symbol, metaphor and analogy. They legitimize new types of activities by finding and linking them to culturally sanctioned analogues. From this perspective we may ask whether charisma can generate a mystique that would legitimize to the population of a new state the massive changes in its ways of life entailed in rapid national development programmes, capitalist or socialist. Our answer would vary, depending on the myths and symbols and the larger body of tradition available for evocation and manipulation. The folk as well as great traditions of Southeast Asia, at least the dominant ones of Indonesia and Burma, seem to offer few if any themes on which to graft the mission of development.

If this is so, then the charismatic founding fathers of these countries were limited in their potential for catalyzing rapid development by virtue of their charisma. They might have directed it to this end more than they seem to have done, but they probably would have had to resort soon to stronger coercive measures than those they employed. And had they resorted to sustained coercion, they might have lost their charismatic hold on both masses and some élites sooner than they lost élite support by their neglect of development.

III

Political Modernization in India

J. C. HEESTERMAN*

CALLOUS though it may seem, crises usually have the advantage for the observer that they bring the social fabric and especially the modes and institutions of leadership into sharp focus. A case in point is the agrarian crisis which developed in the early seventies of the last century in the Deccan and resulted in the Deccan Riots of 1875. This case, moreover, has the added advantage of having been most ably studied by Dr Ravinder Kumar.[1] A variety of factors—a succession of bad seasons, population growth, a boost through increased cotton cultivation during the American Civil War followed by a slump, transfer of land to moneylenders (and presumably rising rich peasants) and the moneylenders' final withholding of credit—contributed to a crisis which was further compounded by the introduction of an increased land revenue demand. Whatever the economic causes, the point of interest for our present purpose lies in the leadership and the ways through which discontent was channelled. On this point Dr Kumar's study is particularly valuable.

* Professor of Indology, Leiden University, The Netherlands.

[1] R. Kumar, *Western India in the 19th Century* (London, 1968), esp. ch. V; also "The Deccan Riots of 1875", *Journal of Asian Studies*, XXIV, 4 (August 1965), pp. 613-37. For a critical assessment cf. M. Charlesworth, "The Myth of the Deccan Riots", *Modern Asian Studies* VI (1972), pp. 401-21.

In the first place the government was petitioned for a revision of the newly introduced assessment rates. Here Dr Kumar interestingly contrasts two different types of leadership and their idioms or modes of expression. On the one hand, we find the local magnate organizing a petition among the cultivators of his locality. The petition is set in the time-honoured mode of broadly and generally evoking the calamities brought on the "helpless poor" by the new assessment rates, contrasting the present misery with a duodecimo version of the golden age, i.e. "the jolly old times in which our fathers swayed the sceptre in prosperity", throwing oneself at the mercy of the benevolent rulers and finally threatening the wrath of "the Almighty God", who "will hear the cries of the afflicted and punish the wicked". Such petitions may have served as a vague sort of danger signal. The government officials, however, would have been all too accustomed to this idiom of protest. It conspicuously failed, as Dr Kumar notes, to bring objective proof of the excessiveness and harmfulness of the new rates.

For this we have to look at a completely different type of document, originating with an equally different type of aspiring leadership, the young brahmin intellectuals who were active in the urban Poona Sārvajanik Sabhā (General Association of Poona). They knew the rational, objective language of political economy and were committed to the ideals that formed this language.[2] In their Report presented to the government in 1873 they used this language to full effect, demolishing the deceptive picture of increased prosperity on which the new rates were based, and demonstrating instead a progressive impoverishment of the peasantry. This Report addressing the government in its own language could not so easily be shrugged off as devoid of objectivity. Moreover—and this seems to have been a matter of concern to the government—here a new type of leadership forcefully announced itself, capable and willing to put itself between the government and the local

---

[2]It may be noted that J. S. Mill was required reading both for logic and for political economy in the Bombay curriculum; see E. E. McDonald, "English Education and Social Reform in Late Nineteenth Century Bombay", *J.A.S.*, XXV, 3 (May 1966), p. 459.

communities, thus threatening to become not only an inter-
mediary but a state within the state. For the Sabhā was not
content with presenting petitions and reports. It tried to
mobilize the peasantry through emissaries who had to enlighten
the peasants and urge them not to pay the new rates. Understandably the government was immediately sensitive to this
potential threat to its authority and tended to identify the
Sabhā's emissaries as the source of trouble wherever it en-
countered difficulties in collecting the new rates.[3]

However, subsequent events showed that the government's
concern about the Sabhā's activities was probably somewhat
exaggerated. For when the crisis came to a head and rioting
broke out in May 1875, there was no sign of any preparation or
organization by the Sabhā. Riots broke out and spread
spontaneously and were directed not against the government
or its agents, but against the moneylenders who were forced—
with a minimum of actual bloodshed or destruction of property
—to give up the bonds and decrees in their possession so as to
obliterate the legal evidence.

[3]Dr Kumar rates the success of the Sabhā in mobilizing the peasantry
as "dramatic" (*Western India in the 19th Century*, p. 180). On balance,
however, it would seem that the impact was greater on the British officers
than on the peasants. Even so the officers quoted by Dr Kumar rather
cautiously "believe" or "have little doubt" that the Sabhā is at the back of
the opposition. A no-tax campaign is a time-honoured way of rural protest
not needing outside organization. The pivotal point is whether this campaign was organized and led locally or centrally directed and co-ordinated.
The Collector of Poona, as quoted by the author (p. 181), speaks of the no-
tax campaign as launched by the Sabhā, but also points to the important
role in it of a few leading landed families, which he unsuccessfully proposed
to subdue. Though there clearly were contacts, or even an alliance, between
urban Sabhā leaders and locally-influential landed families, it seems
reasonable to assume that the real leadership was provided by the latter
which had the monopoly of local influence and which may have used the
Sabhā for their own purposes, rather than allow the Sabhā to encroach on
their preserves. In support of a more sober view of the Sabhā's impact I
refer to G. Johnson, "Chitpavan Brahmins and Politics in Western India"
in E. R. Leach and S. N. Mukherjee (eds), *Elites in South Asia* (Cambridge,
1970) pp. 95-115: "The Sabhā made more attempts than other provincial
associations to unravel the problem of agrarian poverty, but its solutions
were hardly calculated to bring the Maratha peasantry behind its banner."
(p. 115)

II

I have dwelt at some length on the findings of Dr Kumar because they highlight in exemplary fashion the contrast between traditional leadership, organization and idiom and their modern counterparts.

On the one hand, there is the traditional local leadership which for all its ineffective traditional rhetoric showed itself to be quite vigorous and far from eroded by the centralizing tendencies of the British régime. For, even though the British tended to blame the Sabhā's intellectuals for the no-tax campaign, it was also clear to them that the actual leadership that accounted for the vigour of the opposition came from the local magnates. Possibly their influence was also, at least in part, behind the subsequent boycott and final rioting against the moneylenders—perhaps this may even have contributed to the remarkable restraint of the riots. At the very least, it does not seem very likely that they were totally unaware of what was afoot, while it cannot have been totally unwelcome to them to see the moneylenders, who had become a threat to their power, humbled.

On the other hand, we find the urban brahmin intellectuals aspiring to a modern style of leadership, trying their hand at mass political mobilization and concerted action over a wide area. Obviously they were overtaken and bypassed by the development of the crisis, but the British authorities immediately sensed that potentially they represented the ultimate threat to their authority, if not to their immediate power.

At the same time, the capabilities and limitations of both types of leadership become evident. The landed magnates, firmly embedded in the local network of personal relationships, are capable of putting up vigorous obstruction or resistance against the central authorities in ways that are hard to pinpoint and to control. But their effective influence is limited by the extent to which they can maintain personal relationships of a certain density, and is therefore strictly localized. The Sabha, on the other hand, with its branches in the major towns of the Deccan, was in principle not limited to a particular locality but capable of launching clearly-defined actions of a more universal appeal over a wide area. However, it found its limitations in the strongly-entrenched local influence wielded by the rural magnates. Its success or failure depended on the co-operation of these magnates, who of course would hardly have been very prone to allow encroachments on their local preserves.

In fact, the whole episode and its aftermath show the unimpaired resilience of the local communities and their leadership. For, notwithstanding the apparent collapse of the relationship between cultivator and moneylender, the riots pointed up if anything how strongly the two parties depended on each other. And soon after the disturbances we find the local communities successfully trying on their own initiative to settle the differences between the two parties.[4] The traditional organization of society had successfully overcome centralizing pressures and economic strains. There was no room yet for the modern type of supralocal and suprapersonal organization that the young Sabhā intellectuals wanted to offer. Whatever room there was at the time for such an organization was effectively held by the British régime.

III

There can, of course, be little doubt that British rule provided the most powerful early model of political modernity in India. Indeed, that is what the reforming zeal of its Utilitarian designers and inspirers in the first half of the last century wanted it to be. The point is overlaboured and obvious; in fact it is too obvious to be entirely true. At least, it is open to serious qualification as far as its practical impact is concerned. Not surprisingly, the British administrators were themselves the ones who were the most impressed by what they felt to be the destructive impact of their modernizing rule. Especially, the introduction of private ownership of land was felt to have caused "an extensive and melancholy revolution in the landed property of the country", a theme that developed from a prominent subject of discussion in the early nineteenth century into an uncritically accepted dogma. Starting from the assumption of an immutable socio-economic order—an immutability that was both positively valued as the changelessness

4*Op. cit.*, p. 250 *ff.*

of the golden age, exemplified in the romantic cliché of the "village republic",[5] as well as negatively in the sense of stagnation caused by despotism and superstition—they could only view the normal processes through which rights in land changed hands and positions of rural dominance shifted as the sinister outcome of British innovation. When, moreover, these shifts and changes did not seem to give rise to a class of "improving landlords",[6] they understandably took alarm, especially where the beneficiaries were non-agricultural castes, and they tried to salvage what remained of the pristine order of things through legislative action.

For all that, it is at least open to question whether, and if so to what extent, local society was seriously and adversely affected by British rule, let alone the outrageous claims of its wholesale destruction. Cohn's careful studies of the Banaras region[7] suggest a different picture. First, his findings bring out a picture of conflict and forcible dispossession of local landholding lineages, leading to significant changes in land control for at least fifty years before the British began to exercise even indirect influence in the Banaras region.[8] Secondly, as to the question of what happened to those who were dispossessed under the British rules of property, Cohn's cautious conclusion is that "the overall answer may well be that nothing happened".[9] Those who were forced to sell their landed rights changed only their legal status: since they mostly remained in actual possession of their fields, albeit legally as tenants, they could keep their place in the local network of power and influence and from this base effectively resist the demands and encroachments of

[5]On the fortunes of this concept see L. Dumont, "The Village Community from Munro to Maine", *Contributions to Indian Sociology*, IX (1966), pp. 67-89.

[6]The "improving landlord" is, however, not altogether absent, cf. e.g. B. H. Baden-Powell, *The Land-systems of British India* (Oxford, 1892), II, p. 165 *ff*.

[7]See in particular B. S. Cohn, "Structural Change in Indian Rural Society", in R. E. Frykenberg (ed.), *Land Control and Social Structure* (Madison, 1969), pp. 53-121.

[8]*Ibid.*, pp. 57-63. It would seem that such changes were a constant feature in Indian history and not peculiar to the 18th century alone.

[9]*Ibid.*, p. 113.

the new legal owner, especially when the latter, as was often the case, was a town-dweller, who had to act through agents.[10]

As we saw already in the case of the Deccan Riots, the system of local society, being based on personal networks of power and influence and regulated by customs and not by explicit legal formulas, seems to have been but little affected by the British régime. In fact, what stands out clearest seems rather to be the reverse: the eroding impact of local influence working its way up through its connections with the numerous district staff. Here Frykenberg has familiarized us with the image of the white ants silently eating away at the standard of the prestigious imperial umbrella.[11]

IV

It seems fair to conclude that, contrary to the usual assumptions and notwithstanding its own intentions or fears, British rule had only a very limited direct impact on Indian society. This seems the more remarkable as modernity is usually and implicitly credited with an irresistible power of impact. Perhaps the answer can be found not so much in the much vaunted resilience of tradition as in the nature of modernity.

The modernity of British rule, then, consisted in the single-minded commitment to objective rules and methods of government, uniformly to be applied by a centralized bureaucracy. In short, it consisted in a hard-edged conception of the rule of law. It is not that these rules and methods were particularly appropriate to the realities of Indian society. It can easily be argued—as has too often been done, not least by British administrators and judges—that they were not. Paradoxically, their strength may well have been the principled disregard of and refusal to submit to these realities. The rules and methods of the British régime did not derive their legitimation from Indian society—or for that matter from its British counterpart —but from the non-social transcendence of positive written law, a transcendence that was underwritten by the claim that British rules and methods were "scientific" and therefore

---

[10]*Ibid.*, p. 111.
[11]R. E. Frykenberg, *Guntur District (1788-1844)* (Oxford, 1965), p. 231.

absolute. For they were informed by Utilitarian doctrine that trusted in Ricardian political economy as its scientific foundation.[12] This avowedly scientific basis and its rigorous logic meant an absoluteness and universality that was above the contingencies of Indian times and places. Whereas the eighteenth century nabob had marvellously adapted to the Indian environment, the nineteenth century sahib maintained himself by holding on, however tenuously, to absolutes transcending the situational necessities of the environment.

This "scientific" view of the rule of law that provided the British régime with a transcendent legitimation meant that the régime had to keep apart from the shifting sands of local power and influence. Far from destroying local society, it preferred to leave it very much to its own devices. It could only deal with classes of people and legal categories, laboriously and "scientifically" classified in regulations, reports and census, not with actual societies and social relations. Even where it tried to develop a base of popular support in the local magnates as the "natural leaders of the people", it could only endeavour to transform them into an economic category without much social reality, isolating them from the societies they were supposed to lead.

This is strikingly illustrated by the fate of the great landholders or *taluqdars* of Oudh, whose progress from small kings to big landlords has recently been the subject of intensive study.[13] Impressed by the hold exercised by the *taluqdars* over their peasants, who faithfully followed their former masters in the 1857 Revolt, the British understandably decided to turn these "natural leaders of the people" into a powerful support for their régime. Not only were their large estates restored to them, but their ownership was legally strengthened as it never had

[12]See E. Stokes, *The English Utilitarians and India* (Oxford, 1959), esp. p. 80 *ff.*

[13]See T. R. Metcalf, *The Aftermath of Revolt* (Princeton, 1964); the same author's two contributions to R. E. Frykenberg (ed.), *op. cit.*, pp. 123-62; P. D. Reeves, "Landlords and Party Politics in the United Provinces, 1934-7" in D. A. Low (ed.), *Soundings in Modern South Asian History*, (Berkeley, 1968), pp. 261-82, and the editor's introduction, esp. pp. 5-17.

been. In a way the operation was remarkably successful; the *taluqdars* responded by being vocal in their loyalty and praise for their British benefactors, while the British felt that the "coarse looking lot" that the Governor-General had seen at the 1859 Durbar had turned into civilized English gentlemen.

However, notwithstanding the mutual praise and sympathy, the failure of this policy was built in from the beginning, though this became apparent much later under the strains of the twenties and thirties of the present century. For one thing, the *taluqdars* were not a social group, nor could they become one, divided as they were by differences of religion, kinship and marriage. They could only be an economic category—the category of those whose estates paid 5,000 rupees or more in land revenue. More importantly, however, they had exchanged their comprehensive position of local ruler for the narrowly specific one of big landlord, as they discovered to their grief when the 1937 elections made nonsense of their political pretensions.[14]

V

At this point, it may be useful to look into the nature of the "little kingdom" and its ruler in order to understand the change that overtook the *taluqdars*. The latter's fate may thus also illustrate the nature and extent of the modern impact.

First then, the "little kingdom" should not be thought of in strictly territorial terms. This seems to be well illustrated by the elaborate rules for determining—or rather imperatively laying down—the boundaries of villages prior to revenue settlement, although villages "are always known areas distinguished by local names". Not only were the village wastes hardly demarcated if at all, but it could also happen that there was considerable uncertainty whether particular cultivated fields belonged to one village or to another.[15] Moreover, these village boundaries were crossed by lines demarcating estates which might consist of portions of several villages.[16] In Oudh estates

---

[14]P. D. Reeves, *loc. cit.*
[15]See B. H. Baden-Powell, *Land-systems of British India*, II, p. 33 *ff.*
[16]*Ibid.*, p. 30.

interlaced to such a degree that their demarcation was treated
as a distinct branch of settlement work for which a special staff
was employed.[17] Generally speaking, agricultural land was
often divided to an extraordinary degree, according to a genea-
logical or some other customary formula. Thus the cultivated
area was not infrequently found to be parcelled out in a most
intricate way: the tract being divided in four or five blocks or
"villages" (*thok*); this, however, did not mean that each
"village" cultivated its own block, the blocks being divided into
strips of land and apportioned in such a way that "almost every
alternate field belongs to a different one of the four or five
villages". The same principle then governed the further sub-
division in shares, all intermingled. "And yet with this apparent
intricacy", as a settlement officer notes with surprise, "I have
hardly met with a disputed field."[18]

Incidentally, this last example also shows us where the
difficulty lies: the word *thok*, translated as "village", refers both
to blocks of territory and to the branches of the clan or brotherhood. Here the ambiguity surrounding the one-sided definition
and demarcation of the "village" as an administrative territorial
unit stands out clearly. Each "village" block or *thok* is indeed a
known area distinguished by a local name—i.e. the name of the
clan branch—but since each branch has strips of land in all or

[17]*Ibid.*, p. 257.

[18]*Ibid.*, pp. 135-37, referring to Jāt communities on the left bank of
the Jamna. For another example of extreme intermingling of rights in land
that are moreover manifoldly layered, see T. Raychaudhuri's contribution
in Frykenberg (ed.), *Land Control and Social Structure*, pp. 163-74. Though in
this case there certainly seemed to prevail a great confusion about "who
was who and what was whose", resulting in the Settlement Officer's camp
being regarded "somewhat as a lost property office where landlords came
to find their lands and tenants came to find their landlords", it seems
nevertheless to have been a viable system, without major breakdowns. As
the author points out (p. 168 *ff.*) there is no economic explanation for the
proliferation of intermingling rights. It may perhaps be explained in terms
of "investment in people" requiring the accommodation of as great a
number as feasible. The benefits from the resulting interdependence (of
which the fantastic jig-saw of rights in land is only a reflection) are of a
social rather than of a strictly economic nature but of great importance for
the more powerful participants, as is for instance indicated by the economic-
ally meaningless Zimbadari tenure.

most of the other blocks, it is hardly surprising that, at the time of the first settlement surveys, some fields were found to be registered under two villages.[19]

The point I want to stress, however, is that this interlacing of shares and estates reflects the intricate network of personal relations in a "face to face society", not the territorial society.[20] The fact of the matter is that rights in land in such a society are not a matter of individual property, but are primarily regulated by one's membership of and standing in the community that is made up of the personal relations between the sharers as "coparceners" and those between them and their servants. In other words, all are held together by ties of personal inter-dependence of which rights in land are only one, albeit a most important aspect. It is characteristic that the sharers view themselves as a "brotherhood", a group of clan-brethren (or as united by perpetuating marriage alliances),[21] using the idiom of kinship to express their cohesion, and a symbolic number— e.g. four or five *thoks* or *tarafs*, eighteen "forts", eighty-four "villages"—to express their totality.

The intricate web of personal relations and their consequences were intuitively clear to the participants who lived in them—witness the apparent ease with which they handled the complicated system of shares and differential rights in the soil, while highly professional settlement officers had considerable difficulty in understanding their working. Focusing on the single aspect of rights in land, as they had to in order to fix objectively and unambiguously the revenue demand and the

[19]On the face of it, it may seem more surprising that the territorial village unity could be demarcated at all. We should keep in mind, however, the fluidity and adaptability of unwritten custom and customary law, readily responding to changes caused by local conquest, migration, de-population, or expansion, as is abundantly illustrated in Baden-Powell's encyclopædic work. Thus we may find tracts with more compact shares and blocks next to ones characterized by extreme interlacing.

[20]See P. Laslett, "The Face to Face Society" in *idem* (ed.), *Philosophy, Politics and Society* (Oxford, 1956), pp. 157-84.

[21]For the importance of marriage alliance see L. Dumont, *Hierarchy and Marriage Alliance in South Indian Kinship* (London, 1957); for a short statement, "Functional Equivalents of the Individual", *Contrib. to Ind. Soc.*, VIII (1965), esp. pp. 92-94.

persons responsible for its payment, they had to abstract these rights from their social context, the personal relations that constituted the community. The multidimensional web of relations—which it would anyhow be hard if not impossible to fix and record, not only because they were intricate, but also because they were in principle fluid and all the time open to shifts and changes—was left untouched. The revenue settlement could therefore give only a distorted picture of an essentially total situation. Yet it is not likely that, for all the impressiveness of the work involved, it had a decisive impact on the face to face society in the sense of impairing or eroding its system. The reason for this is not so much an extreme concern with preserving existing relations, but the exclusive specificity of the operation itself: it was concerned only with a legal abstraction, rights in land, not with the actual social system and its *modus operandi*, which it left untouched. The area of overlap between legal abstraction and social system was limited and the impingement of the legal system necessarily incidental rather than of an overall nature. In other words, then, the British administrative system provided a fairly loose "husk", covering rather than eroding the little community.

VI

The little community is the essence of the traditional raja and his little kingdom. This means that the ruler derives his power from the local community, that is, from the network of personal relations. In other words, the ruler is part and parcel of the local system of personal interdependence which severely limits his power and freedom of action. In fact, he is often no more than a *primus inter pares* in the midst of his often recalcitrant brethren, who jealously guard their interests and status.

We may take Baden-Powell's description of Rajput organization as an illustration: "The first thing that strikes us is that there is not one sole ruler, but a *series of chiefs*, who, by the exigencies of the case, are graded in a quasi-feudal order and render a certain obedience to the head chief or Maharaja, appearing in the field when required, with a force of foot soldiers or horse, as the case might be. Apart from this, the chiefs really regarded themselves as *coparceners or sharers* with their leader in the kingdom, and retained as much liberty as they could. The Maharaja was the head of the oldest or most powerful *branch of the dominant clan*; the chiefs were the heads of the *other branches or of subordinate clans*."[22]

Power and authority thus seem to be diffused throughout the community—a diffusion that we saw already exemplified in the matter of rights in the soil. The same intricate pattern can also be seen in a traditional system for sharing the agricultural produce at harvest time, known as "division of the grain heap".[23] The intricacies of the system using both proportions and absolute measures are perfectly adapted to the face to face society, since it did not require any aggregate data, and the operation was performed step by step, while all concerned— cultivators as well as servants and village officials—could control each phase of the process. The total result was that, good season or bad season, each received an equitable share according to his place in the community. It is, as Neale terms it, "a redistributive system". For our present purpose, the remarkable point is the position of the raja in this system: he received his share of each cultivator's heap together with servants and village officials, after which a number of pro- portional or absolute deductions were made from the king's share in favour of the cultivator and some servants and village officials.

At the "division of the grain heap" we see the king unam- biguously enmeshed in a complicated web of interdependence. In such a system it is impossible to arrive at any rationality of collection. Owing to the principles of the face to face society to

[22]*Land-systems*, II, p. 324. We may compare L. Dumont's enlightening analysis of a local community of Kallar (*Une sous-caste de l'Inde du Sud: organisation sociale et religion des Pramalai Kallar*, Paris, 1957, p. 141 *ff.*). There we find a quasi-royal lineage that holds a 17th century copperplate charter granting judicial authority. It is unclear whether this lineage ever wielded great power and, anyway, it has sunk into obscurity. At the same time, these Kallar hold that they have no king or chief at all, authority being vested in the "four Tevar" (chiefly lineages), but then every Kallar is Tevar (chief), the title being suffixed to the name of all members of the community.

[23]See W. C. Neale, "Reciprocity and Redistribution" in K. Polanyi *et al.* (eds), *Trade and Market in the Early Empires* (Glencoe, 1957).

which the operation is geared, he has to be present at all the communal threshing floors, of course an impossible requirement. The consequence of all this idyllic rusticity is that not only is it impossible rationally to compute the king's share, but moreover the king has to trust agents, which raises the cost of collection in an equally uncontrollable fashion.

This system, based on interdependence, would seem to go a long way to explain the loyalty exhibited by the subjects in following their small rulers into the 1857 Revolt. But it may equally explain the rulers showing up at the Durbar two years later as a "coarse looking lot", probably but little different from their cultivator subjects. For the king's potential revenues were committed beforehand to a partially uncontrollable, but certainly considerable redistribution. The king was left with little margin, if any, to develop the resources necessary for building up a power base independent from his ties with the community. Even if favourable circumstances permitted an accumulation of resources in the ruler's hands, the redistributive system, through which the network of personal relations had to be kept up, all the time threatened the king's extra resources with dispersal.

VII

Yet, it may be objected, we know of kingdoms or empires spanning large areas or even, as in the case of the Mughal empire, covering almost the whole subcontinent. Prestigious though they may have been, it would seem that in principle they may not have been very different from the little-kingdom system, being held together by personal ties and concomitant redistribution of resources, rather than by a tightly-controlled administrative bureaucracy.[24] The often impressive bureaucracies seem to have been mainly just another redistributive machine. As Pelsaert remarks about the establishment of

[24]With reference to South India, B. Stein states that the well-known empires of Pallavas and Cholas cannot be viewed as centralized bureaucratic polities and that "the Chola state never achieved a command over the resources of the territory it claimed to rule" (in Frykenberg, ed., *Land Control and Social Structure*, pp. 185 & 187).

Mughal nobles: "for the work that could be done by one man, they have ten here."[25]

In this connection the ancient Indian text on the "science" of political economy, Kauṭilya's *Arthasastra*, is particularly enlightening. Its second book draws a much-vaunted picture of an enormous bureaucracy. The first thing that strikes the reader is, however, that there is no indication of a clear-cut hierarchical ordering of the numerous departments. Delegation, lines of command and reporting seem to be unknown. Apparently each of the numerous departments has to be controlled by the king himself, who has to keep up an equally enormous but unorganized body of spies for the purpose. But the real surprise comes in the paragraphs that deal with auditing. Minute regulations are given for the auditing process, but apparently this refers only to the small fry. For the auditing authority is formed by the upper layer of the bureaucracy, the great officers of state or *mahamatras*, among whom we find also the district or provincial collectors.[26] They, however, are not submitted to auditing. Here the unavoidable realities of the situation seem to pierce through the thick layer of theory: the *mahamatras* are not bureaucrats but in fact sharers or coparceners with the king in the realm.[27] The picture that arises from the *Arthasastra*, notwithstanding its clearly opposite intentions, is that of a citadel and city as the centre of the king's power, surrounded by rural districts that are precariously controlled by the king. How precarious this control is becomes clear when Kautilya discusses the relative importance of the different constituent parts (*prakrti*) of the state. Coming to the comparison of fortified royal centre as against rural areas, one authority

[25]F. Pelsaert, *Jahangir's India*, trans. J. Geyl and W. H. Moreland (Cambridge, 1925), p. 55. Perhaps we may in this connection equally think of Frykenberg's description of the British district bureaucracy (Guntur District); the abuses analysed by the author could also be explained in terms of "reciprocity and redistribution".

[26]See H. Scharfe, *Untersuchungen zur Staatsrechtslehre des Kautalya* (Wiesbaden, 1968), p. 229 *ff*.; the relevant passage is *Arthasastra* 2.7, 24-25 (ed. Kangle).

[27]See my "Kautalya and the Ancient Indian State", in *Wiener Zeitschrift fur die Kunde Sud- und Ostasiens* (1972 forthcoming).

concludes that a calamity befalling the city is graver than one befalling the districts. For, as he explains, only the inhabitants of the royal centre are reliable supporters in adversity; the district people, on the other hand, are "common to the enemy".[28]

It would seem that the situation of the Mughal empire was essentially not much different from this general picture. Centred in the Delhi-Agra area, commanding east-west and north-south trade routes and controlling the plains, it could and did muster sufficient resources to achieve preponderance and to give substance to claims of paramountcy. But it was far from being a "territorial society". In fact, it would even be wrong to view the empire as a pyramidal hierarchy, where the higher level controls the lower one. It was not centralized in a vertical way involving clear-cut levels of command and delegation, but rather horizontally, all officers and landholders holding their offices and lands directly from the emperor, who in principle and as far as possible personally controlled all affairs, big or small. In fact, it would seem that the imperial power, for all its undoubted prestige, was in reality only one, though preponderant centre among many other competing and partially overlapping centres, which in varying degrees wielded command over their respective areas and neighbours. In order to keep up and strengthen its ascendancy, it had to obtain extra resources, which, when obtained, threatened to be absorbed by the necessities of redistribution. In other words, it had to keep expanding—or rather it had to keep running in order to stay in the same place. Here the empire had to end up in a vicious circle. Resources had to be found by expansion, but expansion required expenditure. Or, as Athar Ali, dealing with Aurangzeb's annexation in the Deccan, puts it: they "were not the work of a military steam-roller, but of a slow and cumbrous machine, which sought energy and strength by recruiting deserters bribed to come over from the enemy . . . The Deccan involvement led to a great influx of the Deccani nobles into the

---

[28]*Amitrasādhāraṇa; Arthaśāstra* 8.1, 26-27. Kauṭilya himself makes a distinction with respect to the nature of the rural population: if agricultural, then the city is more important; if martial, the rural areas.

Mughal aristocracy".[29] That is, holders of local power and influence had to be enticed one by one to give their allegiance to the emperor by rewarding them with suitable ranks in the imperial service and corresponding grants in land (*jāgīrs*) according to their bargaining strength. The end of the process was that the resources were overstrained, and though service commissions (*mansab*) were still given, there were no more *jāgīrs* to go with them. The process naturally led to a dramatic reduction of the imperial sphere of influence, leaving the field again to the regional and local powers. Whether this indeed meant the total collapse and chaos that is usually associated with the decline of the Mughal power seems to be open to question or at least qualification. Though it would certainly have caused some amount of dislocation, it seems safe to assume that the dislocations caused by the relentless drive for resources for policing the empire were equally, if not more serious. On balance, it would seem that the system of the little kingdom had survived the empire unimpaired. Or rather, the little kingdom had never ceased to be its foundation and basic reality.

VIII

If, after this lengthy digression, we now return to modernity and try to compare it with the little kingdom in its various forms—local sphere of influence, empire and all the shades and levels of power in between—we should be careful not to fall into the trap of all too obvious black and white contrasts. We should be warned already by the fact that, as we have seen, both the pre-modern empire and the modern British raj left the little kingdom system virtually intact. The difference was that, in contradistinction to the system as such, its tangible realizations were more liable to dislocation and disruption by their neighbours[30] than under the British régime, which brought the

---

[29]M. Athar Ali, *The Mughal Nobility Under Aurangzeb* (London, 1966), p. 173.

[30]It would seem that these dangers did not come so much from the imperial power and its officers as from competition for local preponderance between neighbours. At least this is what Cohn's Banaras studies seem to indicate.

over-laboured idea of the immemorial permanence of the "village republic" nearer to realization than it had perhaps ever been.

Further, the Mughals, like the British—who in many respects took their cue from them—strove hard to build up and maintain a rational administration and to regulate and control the assessment and collection of land revenue, both as regards the crown domains and the area given out in *jāgīrs*. They even tried to extend the regulation system to the domains of the great chiefs, who had virtually kept their autonomy, by attempts to change their tribute into rationally assessed revenue.[31] The Mughals certainly did not view their rule as arbitrary despotism, but held on, like their absolutist European counterparts, to a transcendent conception of law. And this was not different from the ancient Indian Kauṭilyan conception of the state, which equally emphasized rational administration, legitimated by the transcendent rule of *dharma*.

IX

The point on which the Mughal empire and its likes had to run aground was, however, the crucial lack of resources needed to free the emperor from the demands of the redistributive system. Having no outside resources, the empire depended solely on the country for its revenues; that is, on the little kingdom, the local sphere of influence through which the revenues had to be realized. In other words, it had to involve itself more and more in the local sphere, becoming progressively more vulnerable to its redistributive demands, which grew with the expansion of the empire and finally overtook it. The harder it strove, the more it became involved in the little kingdom system, till it became itself one. It could not create a new system or a new type of leadership.

On this point, the British position was fundamentally different. Here was an outside power that soon started to expand into a world-wide commercial empire, backed up by the

[31]Cf. S. Nurul Hassan, "Zamindars under the Mughals" in Frykenberg (ed.), *Land Control and Social Structure*, p. 21 *ff.*; on the relevant institution, the *watanjāgīr*, see also M. Athar Ali, *op. cit.*, p. 79 *ff.*

Industrial Revolution. It was, of course, most important for the rising empire that India was part of it, but by the same token British rule in India was not exclusively dependent on the country and its resources, as the Mughals had been. Land revenue certainly remained important for government, but it was not the main support of British power, which had its centre outside India. It could therefore in a way turn its back on the little kingdoms that in the last resort held the key to the country's landed resources, instead of having to involve itself in the quicksands of local influence, where Mughal power had dissolved.

In fact, British rule not only could steer clear from local involvement, but it simply had to, for otherwise local influence would uncontrollably have drained away all power introduced from outside and absorbed it in endless rounds of contests for local and regional preponderance. That this is not an altogether fanciful picture was clearly demonstrated by the runaway confusion after the conquest of Bengal in 1757. Though the uncontrolled British "nabobs" were at the time blamed for the Company's difficulties, it would seem that the malaise lay deeper, in the involvement in the uncontrollable workings of local influence to which the Company's servants enthusiastically adapted, while reaping rich rewards for the atomized elements of extra power which they introduced in the local situations at the Company's expense.

Whatever the influence of the Whig philosophy of government—or, for that matter, the later influence of "scientific" Utilitarianism—the Bengal Code of Regulations of 1793 perfectly fitted the necessities of the British position in India. British power was withdrawn from local involvement by the comparatively simple expedient of rigorously separating the economic benefits of land control from the political power that traditionally went with it. The great landholders were made proprietors of the soil of their estates, but their political capacities, down to the right of keeping armed retainers and of policing their estates, were taken away and exclusively reserved for the government. Whatever the sincerity of conviction, the official statement that "Government must divest itself from the power of infringing . . . the rights and privileges, which . . . it has conferred on the landholders"[32] in practice also meant that the landholders were left to fend for themselves, and that if they were ill-equipped to do so, the government was not to be bothered. No demands could be made on the state, except to the limited extent of upholding the narrowly legal property of the soil. As it turned out, this seemingly simple function of government proved to be endlessly complicated and to over-burden the law courts, but it did not create a drain on the government's power and resources. Permanent settlement, which left a substantial part of government revenues in the hands of the newly-created landlords, was a small price for the obvious advantages.

It is, of course, obvious that British rule was not to be let off quite so easily. Once it started to regulate on one level, it had to go on extending its regulating activity downwards, in a long series of tenancy, indebtedness and alienation acts and in laborious settlement operations. But the underlying concern continued to be withdrawal and reservation of power, including the use of force.

Notwithstanding the unavoidable ramifications of British administration and justice that bored ever deeper into Indian society, the keynote remained throughout steadfast refusal to take the diffuse relations of face to face society into considera-tion, while recognizing only specific relations to which specific rules were to be applied. What in fact were all-inclusive net-works of relations between persons were dealt with in the exclusive terms of the relation between a person and his legal property.

X

As against the particularism of the traditional political system, the universalism of the British régime clearly repre-sented modernity. But here we also see why modern uni-versalism failed to revolutionize Indian society. Government action did not and could not attack on a broad front, but only on specific points. Its effects were therefore only incidental and

[32]Preamble to Regulation II of 1793, quoted by E. T. Stokes, *The English Utilitarians and India*, p. 6.

discrete and could with comparative ease be absorbed and diffused in the traditional all-inclusive system. The *dramatis personae* might change—as they had always done—but the play remained the same.

Thus, for instance, the Oudh *taluqdars* were lifted out of their local context by the strong legal and economic position bestowed on them and upheld by the government. That is, they were no longer dependent on their place in the local network and their ability to manipulate personal relations. Of course, they could convert part of their economic advantages into local influence and pressure, including even use of force, but this was no longer essential to their position, for they did not have to assert themselves any more as leaders of men. From the point of view of the local system, however, nothing much changed. The *taluqdars* had become expendable and the place vacated by them was occupied by other smaller landholders, who saw to it that the system continued as before.[33]

This means that it is not only the inner logic of the British position in India, but the nature of modernity itself that prevented it from having a revolutionizing impact. Modernity and traditional order do not lie on the same even line, but on two essentially different planes. One does not leave the traditional order by the same door as one enters modernity. Modernization, then, is not a matter of the modern order pushing out the traditional order—it does not and cannot—it is a matter of their enduring relationship and its modes and mechanisms.

This unresolved duality, however, is not different from the inner conflict of tradition itself. For if tradition is a lived-in order, bound up with all-inclusive relations and shifting situations, it also has an entirely different aspect. It must provide fixed points, absolute norms, for ordering and legitimating fluid reality. Tradition, therefore, is caught on the horns of an insoluble dilemma: it is situational, but at the same time it should transcend situational flux so as to legitimate it. Nowhere is this clearer than in Indian civilization, where the dilemma

[33]See D. A. Low (ed.), *Soundings in Modern South Asian History*, introduction, p. 15 *ff.*

of tradition was expressed in the form of a peculiarly sharp contradiction. On the one hand, there is the lived-in world of interdependence and complementarity—in short the little community—on the other hand, the transcendent sphere of the ideal brahmin, the renouncer, who breaks out of inter-dependence and denies complementarity. It is the renouncer who holds the key to ultimate legitimation. But here the central contradiction appears: society, being based on interdependence and complementarity, must legitimize itself in terms of a renunciatory idiom that denies society's very basis. Like modernity, transcendent brahmanic (i.e. renunciatory) theory expresses itself in absolute norms and rules that are on a different plane from social reality. Seen in this perspective, it is no matter for surprise that modernization in India can·so often be recognized as brahmanization.[34] For the same reason, the law courts leaned heavily on brahmanic texts. The fact that this tendency rested on a misunderstanding of the nature and applicability of brahmanic law is irrelevant here. The point is that it enabled the law courts "gradually to remove the differentiations of customary law, and bring about a certain amount of manageable uniformity", as a judge of the Madras High Court put it in answer to severe criticisms of the applica-tion of brahmanic law.[35] Even if the nature of brahmanic law had been as well understood from the beginning as it later was, there could hardly have been another way, for it alone carried transcendent legitimation.

It would seem therefore that modernity readily fell into its proper place as a system of legitimation, continuing brahmanic theory. Though modernity and brahmanic theory are more alike in form and structure than in substance, and clearly can-

[34]See M. N. Srinivas, *Caste in Modern India and Other Essays* (Bombay, 1962), chapters I and II.

[35]See L. I. Rudolph & S. H. Rudolph, *The Modernity of Tradition: Political Development in India* (Chicago, 1967), p. 276. The authors argue for "the modernity of Brahmanic law": "Its cosmopolitanism, availability in texts, and cultivation and use by a class of legal specialists, by meshing with the requirements of a national legal system, made it an amenable if some-what delusive instrument for Britons wishing to find and apply a uniform law to Indians." (p. 279).

not be equated *in toto*, the fact that each consisted in discrete elements and not in diffuse totality meant that the differences could be handled piecemeal by means of interpretation in cases of incompatibility, or otherwise by aggregation.

Thus, for instance, the modern constitution, legislation and law courts are committed to equality and therefore do not recognize caste in the sense of hierarchical interdependence and interaction, as it occurs in the little community. But, because they are equally committed to voluntarism and respect for group integrity, they can and do recognize caste in the form of caste associations, educational or religious societies, unions, etc.[36] In other words the modern legal view stresses substance at the expense of relations. In this, it is one with brahmanic theory and brahmanic law that equally reject interdependence. Even though brahmanic theory places the *varṇas* in a hierarchical order, it no less views them as separate, substantive entities while ruling out relations between them, let alone interdependence.

XI

There is, however, one important difference: unlike modernity, brahmanic theory is not tied to a particular sociopolitical order. Indeed it is, as a matter of principle, entirely opposed to any social and political ties. Though this made the realm of ultimate values and legitimation impregnable against political vicissitude, it presented a serious problem for the creation of a modern territorial polity out of the universe of overlapping and competing local influence spheres.

Though British rule did introduce the basic framework of institutions, including public education and finally representative government, it did not of course provide symbols of national identification. As we saw, it did not even erode the little community but rather froze it, while pushing down to the lowest possible level of local rioting and dacoity, its capacity for political expansion. When therefore the British, following

[36]See M. Galanter, "Changing Legal Concepts of Caste" in M. Singer and B. S. Cohn (eds), *Structure and Change in Indian Society* (Chicago, 1968), pp. 299-336, esp. p. 332.

through the logic of withdrawal, started to prepare for Indian self-government and finally independence, the only thing they could achieve was the creation of ever wider arenas for the long-suppressed local and regional factionalism and rivalry.

As always the crucial issues obviously were national identity and national leadership. Now the potential focus of national identity was there all the time, namely the brahmanic ideal of renunciatory transcendence. For nationhood does not require so much a common culture, an uprooted peasantry or even a common territory—these, like other things, can be and, more often than not, are invented—as the common recognition of a transcendent foundation that raises the view beyond the primordial loyalties of face to face society and legitimizes the wider political order. Here, of course, Western political thought could only confuse the issue by its stress on its own brand of secularism, which made the nation itself transcendent—with the catastrophic consequences we know only too well. Thus it remained inconceivable to the British that Hindus and Muslims had to part company, when it came to the realization of nationhood, since Muslims could not share the Hindu view of transcendence and ultimate legitimation.[37] The difficulty, however, was that the Hindu view of transcendence explicitly turned its back on the political order and therefore was not readily amenable to serve it. The question of national leadership could only be the more crucial for it.

It is an article of faith—touchingly adhered to by the international academic community—that in transitional societies members of the intelligentsia are in some way "philosopher-kings: they know, and even their rivals in some way know, that they and only they are fit to rule".[38] But in reality, it seems at

[37]On the role of religion in this respect see L. Dumont, "Nationalism and Communalism", *Contrib. to Ind. Soc.*, VII (1964); French version: *Homo hierarchicus, essai sur le système des castes* (Paris, 1967), pp. 376-95.

[38]See E. Gellner, *Thought and Change* (London, 1964), p. 170. I cannot do justice here to the author's lucid discussion of nationalism, but I cannot help feeling that the intelligentsia as such is rather unfit to gain and wield power, because it has no power base to start from other than the nowhere realm of education and the pursuit of knowledge. At best it may try to resist power—mostly with scant success.

least doubtful that India's new intelligentsia was in any position to provide effective political leadership. Divided as it was by region and community, it was difficult for it to achieve the necessary unity even within itself, while men who achieved prominence on the all-India stage often failed to maintain control of local polities in their home city.[39] Worse still, even their home audiences tended to be restricted to the small well-defined social groups to which they themselves belonged and in which they often had to contend bitterly with their fellows for control. Thus even a redoubtable figure like B. G. Tilak, who would seem to have had at least some of the makings of a charismatic leader, could in his home region hardly reach beyond his Chitpavan Brahmin community and even there he was unable to attain undisputed leadership.[40]

XII

Nevertheless, even when Gandhi did his best to shake their faith, they never had any serious doubt that they and nobody else were the natural leaders of the emergent nation. Thus we already observed them at the very beginning of nationalist politics in the seventies of the last century, making their confident bid for a modern type of leadership, that in fact they thought was already theirs for the taking. But we equally saw that the key to any degree of mobilization lay with the local landed interests. It was only through connections with local magnates that they could hope to make a solid impression. Equally it would seem that the success of the urban Congress intellectuals of the United Provinces not only in ousting the *taluqdars* but, more importantly, in gaining a dominant position on the all-India level, depended to a great extent on their alliance with the smaller Hindu landlords with whom they to some extent overlapped.[41]

[39]For a case in point see C. Dobbin, "Competing Elites in Bombay City Politics (1852-1883)" in E. R. Leach and S. N. Mukherjee, *Elites in South Asia*, pp. 79-95.
[40]See G. Johnson in Leach and Mukherjee (eds), *op. cit.*, pp. 110-15.
[41]D. A. Low, *op. cit.*, p. 12 *ff.*

Such alliances did provide viable and even important bases for political mobilization, but it also meant that they remained essentially dependent on landed interests and their local networks, and even there were not really able to reach the lower strata. So it would seem that no matter how modern their outlook and intentions, they had to work mainly through the traditional type of local-influence politics, and consequently were barred from creating a modern polity.

Perhaps we may even go one step further. It may well be that this was already implied in the nature of their modernity itself. Not because their modernity was alien—as we saw, it falls with relative ease in line with the autochthonous "great tradition"—but because modernity itself is structurally unable to overthrow the particularism of the little community. This made the role of the intelligentsia no less important, but its importance lay in another direction. The intelligentsia provided the necessary linkage between the traditional system of local influence with the modern national polity. Its members can perhaps best be described as the much needed dragomans between the old and the new order. Since, if I am right, we have to consider the uneasy relationship between the traditional and modern orders as an enduring and, we may add, an ever-expanding one, the function of the intelligentsia can only grow in importance. But though it is indispensable and not without political leverage, it is not one of national political leadership or of "philosopher-kings".

Effective national leadership had to come from another quarter, that is, from the sphere of transcendent legitimation, as indeed it did come. I am referring, of course, to Gandhi, whose exceptional charismatic qualities were cast in the mould of the authentic renouncer. Being a renouncer, he could not wield or even touch political power. But whereas the political leader has power, the renouncer, being beyond power and party, transcends it in the most literal sense. His is the absolute authority that enables him to formulate and enforce consensus. He is traditionally the conciliator between the warring parties. Gandhi did not overthrow the traditional order, nor did he have to, but he applied his transcendent authority to the enforcement of national consensus. But it is even more important—and this may well be the mark of his true greatness—that, by rebuilding the nationalist movement into a strong organization that could give full scope to both conflict and to national consensus,[42] he made India's national unity independent of his personal charisma.

Gandhi's crowning achievement would seem to be that he laid the basis for a stable and growing relationship between the lived-in local order and the national state.[43]

In the same way, the problem of leadership and its recruitment came to be solved. Its solution was not solely dependent on the "tall leaders", who had been Gandhi's lieutenants, as the superficial cry, "After Nehru what?" implied. Nor was it solved by installing the intelligentsia as a kind of modern "philosopher-kings". In fact, its members had been the primary victims of Gandhi's non-cooperation and civil disobedience requirements, which either took away their basis of existence or made them suffer the pangs of conscience; in both cases their claim to leadership was undermined. The solution arose naturally from the dual system that was created under Gandhi's ægis. For through the institutional linkages that were first developed in the Congress during the interwar period and later carried over into the national polity, effective new leaders could be and were recruited from the regional spheres into the national consensus-making centre and its governmental arm.

If the cost of maintaining the balance in this multi-centred conciliatory polity may at times seem prohibitive, it also means that, though local or regional disturbances may occur, India's national unity is not really in question. On that basis India can forge ahead without the disruptive upheaval of mass mobilization on a continental scale.

[42]For this dual character of the Indian National Congress and for Gandhi's role in it see D. Rothermund, "Constitutional Reform Versus National Agitation in India, 1900-1950", *J.A.S.*, XXI, 4 (August 1962), pp. 505-22.

[43]Thus, for instance, the modern system of direct elections for the central and state parliaments, based on the individual system, is offset by the local *panchayat* system with indirect vote and giving full scope to the workings of face to face society, while linkage between the two systems is provided by national and state political parties who increasingly use *panchayat* elections as an arena.

One might say that modernity has been "traditionalized"[44] and equally that the traditional order is modernized by its linkage with the national polity, but the essential point would seem to be the stability of their relationship becoming itself an innovatory "tradition".

[44]The expression is R. Kothari's, who concludes that in an "ongoing civilization modernity can survive only by becoming part of tradition, by traditionalizing itself". See R. Kothari, *Politics in India* (Boston, 1970) p. 93; more elaborately in "Tradition and Modernity Revisited", *Government and Opposition* III, 3 (1968). I take the expression in the sense of an expanding linkage between brahmanic "great tradition" and modernity, both changing somewhat in the process.

IV

Leadership and Mass Response in Java, Burma, and in Vietnam*

BERNHARD DAHM†

THE PRESENCE of traditional elements in the thinking of Southeast Asian leadership, exemplified so strikingly in the career of Sukarno,[1] gives rise to questions about the place of tradition in determining the response of colonial populations to the appeals of their leaders and in shaping the character of their struggles for independence. It is proposed in this paper to examine these questions by comparing developments in Java with those in Burma and Vietnam in the period, roughly speaking, from 1900 to 1950. The main reason for the selection of these countries was the considerable strength of the respective independence movements at the end of World War II. How

* A version of this paper appeared in *Solidarity*, VI, 3 (March 1971); acknowledgement is made to the Editor for permission for its reproduction in this volume.

† Scientific Assistant, University of Kiel, Germany.

[1]See my *Sukarno and the Struggle for Indonesian Independence*, translated by Mary F. Somers Heidhues (Cornell University Press, Ithaca, 1969). The sources listed in the following notes concentrate on developments in Burma and Vietnam. For references to developments in Java see the above-named work or my *History of Indonesia in the Twentieth Century* (Pall Mall Press, London, 1971).

was this strength achieved? Was it due to the special capabilities of the leaders just in these countries, or was it the impact of tradition that made the masses respond more readily to their appeals than they did elsewhere? It becomes quickly apparent in these cases that it is not sufficient to discuss only the concepts and attitudes of the leadership which were, as we shall see, not so very different from country to country. To explain the different responses in the three cases, therefore, it will be necessary to enquire somewhat more thoroughly into their religio-cultural background and their traditional social organization.

1. THE TRADITIONAL SOCIETIES

(a) *The religio-cultural background*

At first sight at least, Java, Burma and Vietnam in the cultural sphere seem to be as different from each other as any countries can be. Islam, Buddhism, Confucianism respectively have impressed their religio-cultural values on these societies to such a degree that a newcomer will soon recognize their cultural affiliation. When we look more closely, however, the picture loses its clear-cut features; other elements become visible and seem to play a no less distinctive part in the daily lives of their members, among the reflective few as well as among the unreflecting many.

At the end of the nineteenth century we find in Java and in Burma elements of a surviving animistic and Hinduistic past. The belief in evil and good spirits is still powerful in the villages, and the purists of Buddhism and Islam would discover not a little that is contrary to the teachings of the Buddha or of the Prophet in the religious customs of the people. But since these customs were the way of the ancestors, and, as such, had an important function to perform in the social life of the villages, they were kept alive. So we still find spirit-cults not only in traditional feasts, such as the *slamatans* in Java, but also in official festivals. In Burma, the main festival of the year, the Water-festival, is celebrated in honour of the annual return to earth of the Thagya Min, the king of the *nats*. And there are numerous other examples of spirit-cults, above all in the beloved theatrical performances, the *pwés* in Burma, or the *wayang* or shadow-play of Java. Both might originally have had the function of reconciling the *hantus* or the *nats*, or the spirits of the ancestors which were believed to stay near to their former dwellings.

In the same way, survivals of a Hinduistic past are easy to find in Java and Burma: the presence of Brahmins at the royal courts, for example, with magical functions to perform, such as consecrating the king, finding "safe" dates for important enterprises, and so on. And in the countryside there is the great Indian mythology, from which the *wayang* and the *pwé* borrowed their topics and a large part of the population their ethical maxims.

A common animistic and Hinduistic past thus serve to bring Java and Burma closer together. But there is more which relates the two countries to each other. Java had also undergone a Buddhist phase before Islam became the dominant religion of the island. There were, of course, aspects of the teachings of the Buddha and Muḥammad which resembled each other. Both taught the vanity of this life, both taught the way of individual salvation. And in both Java and Burma there were religious schools in or near almost every village. In Burma, there were the *pongyi-kyaungs*, in which the Buddhist monks taught the village boys the precepts of the Buddha: how to gain merit, how to improve their *karma*, how to achieve *Nirvāna*. In Java there were the *pesantren*, where the *kyais* or religious teachers taught the *Qur'ān*, the *Sunna* and the way to Paradise. Finally, in Java and Burma there were ancient messianic traditions predicting the arrival of a just prince who would bring an age of plenty, the Ratu Adil in Java, the Setkya Min in Burma. These traditional beliefs could find echoes in the Mahdi and Maitreya speculations respectively. Thus the people in Java and Burma had both the hope of a sudden improvement of their lot in this life and, if the Messiah did not come, the prospect of salvation in the life hereafter.

In Vietnam it was different. As will be shown below, there were some Bodhisattva speculations in Vietnam too, but Buddhism there had lost its soteriological aspects. Instead, it was imbued with magical rites. Those who wanted to become

monks had to pass crucial tests, the fire-test for instance, in
which they had to carry burning coals on their shaven heads.
And there were other magical practices, so that the saying
went: "A Vietnamese with self-respect does not become a
bonze".[2] The reason for the little esteem in which the Buddha's
teachings were held in Vietnam lay with the mandarins. They
had fought the soteriological aspects of Buddhism as a possible
challenge to mandarin rule. From the beginning, there had
been periodic persecutions of monks and destruction of pagodas
in China and in Vietnam, the last one in Vietnam being that
which occurred under the Tay-Son at the close of the eighteenth
century.[3]

Emperors and mandarins placed no store by a gospel that
preached individual salvation. They were interested rather in
maximum exploitation which was best provided for by communal acts. Thus, the communities had to be strengthened and,
in the course of time, religion too became a community affair.[4]
The smallest communities, the families, had their ancestor-
shrines; the larger community, the village, had its *dinh*, or local
genius, who was revered commonly in the community-hall,
also called the *dinh*; the kingdom, finally, had its state genii,
among whom, besides three others, was the Buddha. The
prospects of individual salvation were thus suppressed, and
messianic aspects were ridiculed. The man who wanted to
escape from ordinary life could resort to magical practices.

[2]E. Langlet, *Le peuple annamite: ses mœurs, croyances et traditions* (Berger-
Levraut, Paris, 1913), p. 55.

[3]M. Weber, "Konfuzianismus und Taoism" in *Gesammelte Aufsätze zur
Religionssoziologie*, Bd. I (Mohr, Tübingen, 1922), pp. 448, 462, 501;
Langlet, *op. cit.*, pp. 53-54; G. Dumoutier, *Le Grand-Bouddha de Hanoï:
étude historique, archéologique et épigraphique sur la pagode de Tran-Vu* (Schneider,
Hanoi, 1958), p. 42. For a general discussion of Buddhism in Vietnam at
the time of annexation see also G. Dumoutier, *Les symboles, les emblèmes et les
accessoires du culte chez les Annamites: notes d'ethnographie religieuse* (Ernest
Leroux, Paris, 1891) and P. Giran, *Magie et religion annamites: introduction à
une philosophie de la civilisation du peuple d'Annam* (Augustin Challamel, Paris,
1912).

[4]Weber, *op. cit.*, Ch. VI, "Konfuzianische Lebensorientierung",
pp. 430-58, brilliantly discusses the reasons for the absence of messianism,
eschatology and soteriology in China.

He could try to prolong his life by sorcery, he could join a
secret society, or become a bonze, but he would always be
regarded as a parasite. For the great majority of the Vietnamese, however, if conditions became unbearable, or if they
wanted a change, there was only one alternative left: to take
up arms and fight.

(b) *The Social Organization*

Let us now glance at the social organization of our respective
societies. Here again, before the arrival of the Europeans, we
find a close resemblance between conditions in Java and
Burma. In the palace-city ruled a semi-divine king, the
supreme authority in every field. He could declare war, he
could decide matters of life and death, he appointed his
ministers and provincial governors. Around him there were a
number of queens and sycophants, who had survived the purge
of potential rivals with which every ruler began his reign. The
people tolerated him since he obviously had the strongest
karma or whatever justification there was for his claim to rule.

From the time of their appointment, the governors were
vested with supreme power in the provinces. The *wuns* in Burma
or the *bupatis* in Java had to satisfy the material wishes of the
ruler and his entourage as well as their own personal ambitions
as long as they had a chance to do so. In the countryside they
were helped by the semi-hereditary administrative corps, the
myothugyis in Burma, or the *priyayis* in Java—the men who
contacted the villages, collected the taxes, and, in times of war,
recruited the soldiers. In the villages a group of elders decided
how to levy the taxes and various other claims on the people.
At the grass-roots we thus find at least some democracy. But it
must be noticed that in the villages too there were the privileged
few and the unprivileged many. The former could be retired
administrative officials, or those who had earned merit in a war,
or who could prove that they were descendants of the founders
of the village. Newcomers usually had no rights at all.

At the village level things were not very different in Vietnam.
Here too we find semi-independent units with probably an
even stronger sense of communal bonds. Whereas in Burma it
often happened that a peasant left his village if he heard of

better conditions somewhere else,[5] in Vietnam, where the village was usually surrounded by a bamboo fence, people preferred to stay put. They had some claims to protection from the local genius, they waited at *tet* (New Year) for the visits of the spirits of ancestors who might not find them if they had left, and they felt safe from arbitrary measures by the mandarins.

The institution of the mandarin system is thus the one feature which distinguishes the social organization of Vietnam from that of its Southeast Asian neighbours. On the administrative level as on the cultural level the impact of a thousand years of Chinese supremacy had been complete. The mandarin's career was open to every one. In the villages there were schools, not led by religious teachers as in Java or Burma but by retired mandarins of a lower rank. Gifted boys could proceed to the next district town and try to qualify for the triennial examination. Those who passed with distinction could go further, and the élite of the country met at Hué for the doctoral examination. The subjects taught were Chinese classics, literature and ethics. There was no modern science or technology.

The successful candidates would receive the key positions in the state. Their qualification thus depended not on the benevolence of the king, as was the case in Java or Burma, but on their diplomas. This meant that in practice the mandarins, in the military as well as in the administrative field, were much more self-reliant than their colleagues in Java or Burma could ever dare to be. The king, if he was not a strong character, could easily come under the tutelage of ambitious mandarins. It was only in the state-preserving cult that his authority was unquestioned.

We have already noticed the role the mandarins have played in depriving Buddhism of its dangerous soteriological aspects. A similar fate would meet any other potential threat to their rule. Thus the mandarins recognized as early as the beginning of the seventeenth century the danger of Christian missionaries and they issued decrees forbidding the "foreign barbarians" to

[5]F. S. V. Donnison, *Burma* (Ernest Benn, London, 1970), p. 68 *ff.*, quoting from C. H. T. Crosthwaite, *The Pacification of Burma* (E. Arnold, London, 1912), pp. 5-6.

seduce the "simple people" or "to corrupt good manners" by spreading their "perverse religion".[6]

2. THE IMPACT OF COLONIAL RULE

It was in the second half of the nineteenth century that the impact of European powers was felt decisively for the first time in our respective societies. By this time traders and missionaries had been active in Southeast Asia for at least three hundred years; and in the case of the Philippines the Europeans had even succeeded in totally dominating an Oriental people. The missionary zeal of the Spaniards had managed to Christianize the central islands almost completely within decades. And the result shows the significance of cultural domination. When revolutionary trends became articulate in the late nineteenth century the demands resembled Latin American claims rather than those which were heard in other parts of Asia at the same time. This was true for the brains of the movement, for Rizal, for Marcelo del Pilar, for Mabini, but it was also true for Andreas Bonifacio and his Katipunan, built on the model of Freemasonry rather than on the model of Chinese secret societies.

The Dutch traders who had come to Java in the early seventeenth century had been less interested in spiritual gains. After having subdued the Javanese nobility, they were satisfied with putting the *bupatis* to their own cart and kept themselves aloof from the villages. Here it was only in the middle of the nineteenth century that the European impact was directly felt— when the Dutch ordered the Javanese peasants to use a fifth of their land for crops for which a demand existed in the European market. This was a more severe encroachment upon peasant rights than had been the occasional attempts to interfere in the management of village affairs since the beginning of the century. After the abolition of what was called the *cultuurstelsel* or cultivation-system in the 1860s, free-trade concessions and a *laissez-faire* policy made things worse for the Javanese masses: with encumbrance, mortgaging, money-lending, interest and compulsory labour, the screw of misery had started to turn.

[6]P. Isoart, *Le phenomene national vietnamien: de l'indépendance unitaire a l'independance fractionnee* (Pichon et Durand-Auzias, Paris, 1961), pp. 84-95.

When, after three wars in 1825, 1852 and 1885, Burma was annexed to Britain's Indian Empire, the break with the past was sharper than in Java. Nominally at least, the princes of Central Java had retained their authority and some special rights. In Burma, the king was deposed and exiled. Burma became a province of British India. The traditional system of self-government at the village and township level was abolished. A highly-centralized administration with direct rule was introduced, severe taxation and individual responsibility were decreed, a new code of law and a new educational system followed suit.

The French, who conquered Vietnam in the period 1860 to 1885, might at the beginning have intended to follow the Dutch pattern rather than that of the British. The fierce opposition they met after they had occupied the South, later known as Cochin China, and the flight of the mandarins to the North, left them little choice but to introduce direct rule. After the subjection of the rest of the country, the French created the protectorate of Annam in Central Vietnam and the protectorate of Tongking in North Vietnam, thus dividing the country artificially into three parts. In Indonesia and Burma, colonial rule, despite protective measures or minorities, helped to create the future nation states, which in the past had hardly had a national identity. In Vietnam a nation which had fought for centuries for its unity, and had achieved it at last under emperor Gia Long in 1801, was again torn apart with, as we know today, disastrous consequences. And even if it is claimed today that the creation of Cochin China as a special unit had some justification in that it was practically a reinforcement of the age-old cleavage between North and South,[7] it must also be emphasized that at the moment of the French conquest, and

[7]See, for instance, John T. McAlister Jr, *Vietnam: The Origins of Revolution* (Allen Lane, The Penguin Press, London, 1969), pp. 40-45. In my opinion, however, the particularity of the South before the French arrival should not be over-emphasized. Similar circumstances existed in Burma between the upper and the lower part of the country and they did not provide an obstacle in the process of nation-building. Moreover, there was not the highly-effective central administration that we find in Vietnam in pre-colonial days.

for two generations at least, the country had been united under a highly-effective administration. Captain Gosselin, a participant in the French conquest, claimed that, "From the mountains in Upper Tongking down to the frontiers of Cambodia we have found the most united people one could imagine from the ethnic, political and cultural point of view".[8]

In the field of administration, Cochin China, which became a colony, underwent a fate similar to that of Burma. The traditional communal bonds were undermined by the introduction of individual taxation and responsibility. In Tongking and Annam, where the traditional administration was retained, the strict French supervision and the regular registration of births and deaths, which provided excellent tax-rolls, had, in fact, the same effects.[9]

Further departures from the traditional ways, in Vietnam as in Java or in Burma, were, of course, effected by economic measures. The introduction of the monetary system, wage-labour, coolie recruitment for the estates of foreign planters, high interest on loans and money-lending, these all led to a change of traditional habits and to an increasing radicalization of the people. Those who could make their profit under the prevailing conditions were few. For the masses, all these new institutions meant nothing but exploitation.

3. THE EMERGENCE OF A NEW LEADERSHIP

The immediate response to the institution of colonial rule in Burma and Vietnam was the same. As soon as people realized the foreigners had come to stay, they armed themselves with lances, swords, bamboo sticks, amulets and the like and started to fight. Reckless resort to wholesale executions, extortion and pillage of villages by the Europeans at first only contributed to the spread of rebellion. Here and there the intruders had to call in additional troops to quell the nation-wide, though badly-organized resistance. Local leaders and the princes of

[8]Ch. Gosselin, *L'empire d'Annam* (Perrin, Paris, 1904), p. 7.
[9]P. Mus, "The Role of the Villages in Vietnamese Politics", *Pacific Affairs*, XXII (1949), p. 226.

the ruling dynasties gained a strong following until the so-called pacification was achieved.

The furious, though hopeless fight in Burma and in Vietnam after annexation was also the death-agony of the traditional élite. After the defeat, the social organization of old was irrevocably gone. The resistance leaders were either killed or exiled. Their colleagues who sought jobs with the new masters soon saw their authority challenged. They were criticized by those who understood how to express, by more efficient means, the lasting opposition of the people to foreign domination.

The new élite which emerged under colonial rule, and this is true for all three countries under consideration, might roughly be divided into four categories: the *careerists*, the *associationists*, the *constitutionalists* and the *revolutionaries*. The careerists were the job-hunters, those who sold out to the foreigners in order to achieve personal gain. They were the favourites of the colonial power; they could be used for all ends and had no inconvenient claims. Though they played an important role in the colonial era, they never became leaders in the proper sense of the word. They were despised by all sectors of the population much more than were the collaborating traditional élite which, after all, had only bowed to *force majeure*.

The new leadership was to be found among the three remaining categories. The associationists and the constitutionalists form a group apart. In contrast to the revolutionaries, they might be called the compromisers. They were indeed ready to accept colonial rule for a span of time, though they never sold out to the colonial power. The associationists, mainly descendants of privileged classes of former times, sought to build a bridge between East and West and between past and present, trying to modernize their own traditional concepts or trying to adapt others. But they were concerned to preserve their society as it was. To this group belong cultural societies, such as the Young Men's Buddhist Association, founded in Burma in 1906 for the first ten years of its existence, or, in Java, *Budi Utomo*, founded in 1908, after the higher *priyayis* had pushed aside a revolutionary group around Tjipto Mangunkusumo. In Vietnam, Pham Quynh, author of the *Essais franco-annamites*, and his affiliates would fit into this category. The associationists took second place in the hearts of the colonialists, since they came close to an ideological justification of colonial rule as a sacred mission.

The constitutionalists were inclined to follow Western concepts more closely. They were the better-educated and hoped by copying the way of their masters to find more understanding for their demands in the respective mother-country. And these demands included the grant of the liberal freedoms, encouragement of an indigenous industry and self-government. They were the emerging bourgeoisie and wanted to supplant some day their colonial rulers in the political and economic fields. In each of our countries we see such constitutionalists: in Vietnam it was the "Constitutionalist Party" of Bui Quang Chieu, in Burma it was the "Twenty-One Party" and its successors under U Ba Pe, and in Java it was Dr Sutomo's *Partai Bangsa Indonesia* which, in 1935, united with *Budi Utomo* and formed the *Partai Indonesia Raya* or *Parindra*.

Whereas the associationists and the constitutionalists did not care too much about the people and had, in fact, not much in store for them, the revolutionaries knew that the masses alone could put the necessary pressure behind their demands. And they were not satisfied with self-rule or autonomy. In contrast to the other groups, they had no stake in the present structure of society. They had been educated for the implementation of the orders of the colonialists. They were the teachers, the vaccinators, engineers and office-clerks and had been offered only an inferior social rank. Thus they wanted a change in the structure of society too. But how to rally mass support for their demands? The masses after all still stuck to their tradition.

We see a variety of kinds of effort. There were the preachers, some preaching outright a holy war against the foreign invaders, others calling for boycott and resistance, not to buy foreign goods, not to pay taxes and so on. Others again tried to mobilize the masses by claiming that traditional values were in danger, or by contrasting a fictitious golden past and an even brighter future with the present hardships. And there were the organizers: some trying to apply Western revolutionary tactics such as cadre-building or underground activities, others demanding education first, fighting against superstition and so on. How did the masses respond to all these activities? Was there any method among the many tried, which proved to be especially successful? Was it the preachers or the organizers who triumphed in the end? Was it the charismatic leaders, such as Tjokroaminoto or Sukarno in Java, U Oktama or Aung San in Burma, Phan Boi Chau or Ho Chi Minh in Vietnam? Of course, they kept the fancy of the masses busy. But why— what was their charisma? It was that they consciously, and more often unconsciously, acted in accordance with their own religio-cultural tradition.

4. MASS RESPONSE IN JAVA

In Java, as we have seen, the impact of colonial rule was first decisively felt among the masses in the middle of the nineteenth century. And at this time we note a distinct decline in the authority of the *priyayis*, who had for a long time been subject to the Dutch. Now people began to curse their once-respected leaders. In former times they had had the right to complain at the princely court in cases of arbitrary exploitation. Peasants, either individually or in groups, could try, by exposing them-selves to the glittering sun in front of the palace, to provoke the compassion of the prince. He then might have listened to their complaints and might have punished the evil-doers.[10] But these times were gone; the Dutch would not be moved by com-passion and the *priyayis* had no punishment to fear.

At about the same time as we notice a decline in the authority of the traditional élite, an Islamic revival made itself felt in Java. The teachings of the *kyais* in the *pesantren* became dis-tinctly more Islamic. Many of them now, after the opening of the Suez Canal in 1869, had a chance to make the pilgrimage to Mecca. That voyage, before a hazardous enterprise, was now easy, since European steamboats on their way to Europe could take the pilgrims straight to the holy places. And the pilgrims returned home not only with a new esteem for the teachings of

---

[10]B. J. Haga, *Indonesische en Indische Democratie* ("De Ster", The Hague, 1924), p. 126 *ff.*

the Prophet, but also with a sense of a growing solidarity in the world of Islam and with a more critical attitude towards the unbelieving foreigners and their administrative tools.[11]

Thus there was a growing discontent among the Javanese masses. They saw their rights ignored, a proportion of their crops taken away and sometimes even their fields which were theirs by ancient custom. In West Java, where Islam had its strongest hold, the peasants revolted in 1888, and there were 47 deaths, among them Europeans and native officials.[12] In East Java, in the 1890s we see a peasant, Samin, instigating a large group of people to refuse to pay taxes, to ignore government orders and to lead a life of their own. The group even had its own religion, the religion of Adam. And if the rest of Java was quiet, the Dutch did not feel at ease. They had found, circulating among the masses, a number of the *surat Djajabaja* or prophecies of Jayabaya. This king of olden times allegedly had prophesied the arrival of the Dutch but also their departure, depending on the advent of the Ratu Adil, the Messiah, who would turn wrong into right, lack into abundance, misery into happiness. Islamic Mahdi expectations had intensified this messianic tradition, which originated in Buddhistic Maitreya speculations.

According to the circulating versions of the prophecy, the great event was not far away. The signs that the time was close could easily be recognized. God himself would pave the way for the Messiah and destroy his enemies. Why therefore was there any need to fight? People had only to wait, to watch the signs, to learn the formulas and discover how to welcome the deputy of God. The belief was so intense that in various parts of Java pretenders arose, claiming to be the Ratu Adil and causing no little concern to the local administration. People had then begun to speculate and to wait for greater things. Another factor which strengthened this reflective passivity was the *wayang*, the

[11] See, for instance, the memoirs of the Javanese regent, A. Djajadiningrat, *Herinneringen* (G. Kolff, Amsterdam, 1936), p. 20 *ff.*, where he recalls his own life in a *pesantren*.

[12] For details see S. Kartodiradjo, *The Peasants' Revolt of Banten in 1888: Its Conditions, Course and Sequel*, Verhandelingen van het Koninsklijk Instituut voor Taal-, Land- en Volkenkunde, L (1966).

shadow-play, with its constant assurance that those who do right will find justice, and that the evil-doers will be punished, even if it takes some time. Thus again: Why fight? This attitude of reflective passivity, of wait-and-see, is indeed characteristic of the Javanese people. The many speculations which occupied the fancy of the illiterate rural population created at the same time an atmosphere of would-be revolutions and of general passivity.

This was the experience of the revolutionaries too, after they had started their agitation. The masses were sympathetic to their demands, but they kept aloof. There were times, as in the early days of the *Sarekat Islam* when they came *en masse*, in order not to miss the chance of buying a membership-card to what to them seemed to be the organization of the Ratu Adil. There was again an unruly time in 1929-30, when they thought something extraordinary would happen, and again shortly before the outbreak of the Pacific War, when they knew the rule of the Dutch was doomed. But whenever the revolutionaries tried to organize the masses, tried to transform them, as Sukarno frequently put it, into a *banjir* ("a flood"), an irresistible torrent which would drive the Dutch out of the country, they were frustrated in their hopes. The most daring of them would become the heroes of the people. Allusions to the prophecies and *wayang*-topics could temporarily arouse passions and could do away with the myth that the people were satisfied with Dutch rule. But by this very means the attitude of wait-and-see was merely strengthened.

The alternative way of mobilizing the masses—by applying Western revolutionary tactics, such as cadre-building and working in the underground, as tried by the PKI or Sjahrir's Fabian Socialists—met with even less success. These attempts found little response among the people but much attention on the part of the colonial power. When the latter in the 1930s had the revolutionaries exiled, the independence movement was virtually dead. Up to the arrival of the Japanese a few parties, led mainly by the constitutionalist-type leaders or by religious reformers, remained on the scene, it is true, but their total membership did not amount to 1 per cent of the forty million Javanese. Thus it was only in the Japanese occupation period that things changed. It was the Japanese war-machine which created the Indonesian army and the *pemuda* groups which at the end of the war were wildly determined to fight, either the approaching Allies or the Japanese themselves. It was under the Japanese that the revolutionaries got free access to the masses and that the latter were startled out of their passivity both by national appeals and by the stern measures of the occupation forces. It was the first, and, as I see it, the only time that the Javanese masses were ready to become involved in political action. And not for long. As soon as things were normalized, passivity returned.

To put it bluntly, it may be doubted whether a political evolution of the masses has occurred even in the subsequent period of independence and intense party activity. It is a fact that more than three million members of the PKI did not fight in the crucial days of October 1965. There was as little support for the Communists then, as there had been in 1926 when the PKI had made its first bid for power, or in 1948 when it made its second attempt. Nor was there any significant protest against the step-by-step deposition of Sukarno and the reversal of his policies. There was instead much speculation about the secret powers of the new leader who had been unknown before 1 October 1965.

Sometimes, it may seem as though the masses are watching the actors on the political scene, as they watch the shadows on the *wayang*-screen, believing them to move in accordance with a godly plan, as the puppets move in accordance with the plans of the *dalang*, the revered puppet-player. Sometimes, they are startled by political uproar, as they are, at a *wayang*-performance, by the noisy sounds of the usually tuneful *gamelan*-orchestra. But, in general, they are waiting for the dawn when, in the world of *wayang*, the evil forces are finally destroyed.

5. MASS RESPONSE IN BURMA

In order to grasp the different mentality of the Burmese, it is worth staying for a moment on the ground of theatrical performances. Sir George Scott, writing in 1882 about the *zat pwé*, the national passion of the Burmese, said:

> There is no nation on the face of the earth so fond of
> theatrical representations as the Burmese. Probably there
> is not a man otherwise than a cripple who has not at some
> period of his life been himself an actor, either in the drama,
> or in a marionette show, if not in either of these certainly
> in a chorus dance. It would be wrong to say that there is
> no other amusement in the country but it is indisputable
> that every other amusement ends up with a dramatic
> performance.[13]

And F. S. V. Donnison, the long-time Chief Secretary of the
British Government in Burma, comments on the *pwé* in his
recent book:

> Here is something essentially Burmese, romantic,
> humorous, irreverent, enormously vital.[14]

"Every Burmese an actor", "enormously vital". There is
here indeed a different mentality which can also be noticed in
political life. We have mentioned the fierce resistance the
Burmese waged against the British and we will notice it again
in the course of the struggle for independence. Why then did the
opposition against British rule after the national outburst calm
down? Donnison suggests that the people were tired of fighting,
but also that they had learned their lesson, that they simply
could not stand up against the British forces.[15] In Vietnam,
however, under much the same conditions, fighting continued.
What else could have stopped fighting in Burma?

I think the decisive factor was Buddhism. In a number of
recent books, writers have maintained that the *pongyis* in their
yellow robes led the fight against the British.[16] It may be

---

[13]Shway Yoe (Sir James George Scott), *The Burman, His Life and
Notions* (Norton, New York, reprint 1963), p. 286.

[14]F. S. V. Donnison, *Burma*, p. 225.

[15]*Ibid.*, pp. 76, 92.

[16]See, for instance, D. E. Smith, *Religion and Politics in Burma* (Princeton
University Press, Princeton, 1965), p. 85; H. Bechert, *Buddhismus, Staat und
Gesellschaft in den Ländern des Theravada-Buddhismus*, Teil 2, "Birma, Kam-
bodscha, Laos, Thailand" (Harrassowitz, Wiesbaden, 1967), p. 100.

doubted whether this is true. There might have been exceptions, but in Upper Burma at least the monks preached peace instead of war. It is rather symptomatic that U Oktama, the well-known resistance leader in the 1880s, had left monastic life before he took up arms.[17] *Pongyis* involved in the fighting all lived in Lower Burma,[18] which at this time had already been for thirty-five years under British rule with effects on Buddhism which will presently be noticed. In Upper Burma, according to the account of Fielding-Hall, who was there when the rebellion broke out, the *Sangha*, the hierarchical, structured organization of the monks, kept totally aloof from the uprisings. Fielding-Hall even wonders what might have happened to the British, if the monks had indeed become the leaders of the rebellion.[19]

In Upper Burma in the 1880s the *Vinaya* rules, the code of conduct for monks, still curbed the temptation of the monks to get involved in political affairs. This code, which under King Mindon Min had been newly drawn up, obliged the *pongyis* to conform strictly with the teachings of the Buddha not to mingle in worldly matters, not to kill but to preach peace in unruly times. And this is what the *pongyis* did. The British, however, were not grateful to the *Sangha*. They considered it a potential threat to their authority and severely restricted the powers of the *Thathanabaing*, the head of the *Sangha*. In Burmese times, the *Thathanabaing*, who was appointed by the king, could enforce discipline among the monks. There was a state commissioner, the *Mahadanwun*, who acted on his advice. The latter could, if disciplinary measures taken by the abbot of a monastery were not sufficient, unfrock the monk and hand him over to a secular trial. This system was abolished by the British. They furthermore deprived the *pongyis* of their educational function, if the latter were not willing to conform with the schemes of the education department. Thus the British did

[17]E. Sarkisyanz, *Buddhist Backgrounds of the Burmese Revolution* (Nijhoff, The Hague, 1965), pp. 104-5.

[18]J. F. Cady, *A History of Modern Burma* (Cornell University Press, Ithaca, 1958), pp. 130, 137, 139-40.

[19]H. Fielding-Hall, *The Soul of a People* (Macmillan, London, 1898), pp. 56-59, and *A People at School* (Macmillan, London, 1906), p. 138.

their best to encourage the disintegration of the *Sangha* and paved the way for the political monks who mobilized the masses in the 1920s.

These political monks did not come overnight. It took some thirty-five years, one monk-generation, as before in Lower Burma, until they openly dared to disregard the *Vinaya* rules and to disobey their superiors, or the *sayadaws*, the learned experts of the *Tripiṭaka*, the law and rules and ethics of Buddhism. It was a slow process until the scruples were overcome that they might affect their *karma*. The man who did most for the radicalization of the monks was another U Oktama, who was a boy of eight when the old resistance leader was shot in 1880. He had studied in India, and for five years in England and France. After the Russo-Japanese War, he had gone to Japan to study the secrets of the latter's power. Since then he was convinced that what was needed was mass agitation. During World War I he was under house-arrest in Mandalay. When, in 1920, he saw the people's response to the students' strike he decided to act. The best means to mobilize the masses was for him to mobilize the *pongyis* first. Those who once had preached peace now should preach resistance.

Even if U Oktama agitated in a monk's robe, I cannot, as Sarkisyanz and others did,[20] regard his activities as an attempt to modernize Buddhism. There is little evidence for the theory that he preached the pursuit of *Nirvāṇa* in this world, or that he tried to turn the quest for deliverance from universal suffering into a quest for deliverance from social needs. He should be seen rather as a revolutionary, the preacher-type, who wanted to get rid of British rule by appealing to traditional values. He preached that the law of the Buddha could not be obeyed, as long as there was foreign rule in Burma. He said there was no chance of salvation, no attainment of *Nirvāṇa*, as long as people lived in slavery. He criticized the *sayadaws* for being interested only in the *Tripiṭaka*; they should study subjects of greater importance, such as history, economy and sociology. And he told the monks that they should, with their alms-bowls, not only ask for their daily needs, but should also go to the foreign

[20]E. Sarkisyanz, *op. cit.*, pp. 125-27.

masters and ask for the return of the country.[21]

The monks understood. Throughout Burma, within a few years, the villages were again mobilized. In the towns the various factions of the General Council of Burmese Associations wooed *Sangha*-support on the occasions of elections and so on. In the countryside, village-organizations, the *athins*, grew in opposition to the official administration. People refused to pay taxes in all parts of the country and the monasteries became a hotbed of agitation. The result was, as in Java at the same time, that prophecies came alive. Here it was the Setkya Min, derived from Aśoka's Cakkavattin idea, the ideal ruler of the future, closely related, as Sarkisyanz has shown, with Maitreya speculations.[22] The Setkya Min was to prepare the way for the coming Buddha, in theory still far away, but not so in the speculations of the people. There had been pretenders at all times, but now that his arrival was preached in the villages, things got out of control. In Java in 1929-30 widespread rumours led to nothing but passive speculations. In Burma they led to a country-wide rebellion, after Saya San had himself proclaimed king in December 1930, and they lasted for some twenty months, claiming thousands of lives.

After this disaster, the political élite, associationists, constitutionalists and revolutionaries alike, tried to curb the activities of the political monks. After they had exploited the rebellion for their own political demands, their interest concentrated on what the British had in store for them, the new constitution, which was inaugurated in 1937. This constitution gave, nominally at least, governmental powers apart from foreign policy, defence and finance, into Burmese hands. Thus many of the activities and jealousies which had formerly been directed against the British, now concentrated on this governor-controlled *pwé* in Rangoon. But whenever mass support was

[21]Accounts of U Oktama's activities are given in D. E. Smith, *op. cit.*, pp. 95-99, and in F. v. d. Mehden, *Religion and Nationalism in Southeast Asia* (University of Wisconsin Press, Madison, 1963), pp. 134-36, 213-14. The foregoing is based, however, on unpublished material, consulted in the India Office, London. The sources will be mentioned in a forthcoming study.

[22]Sarkisyanz, *op. cit.*, p. 86 *ff.* and 149 *ff.*

needed, it could easily be gained: in the Anti-Muslim riots in 1938, in the strike movement of 1939 and the like. When in the course of the war the Thakins, almost unknown up to 1941, made an appeal to the people to join their Anti-Fascist People's Freedom League, it instantly became a powerful weapon.

One wonders, therefore, why Communism did not gain significance before independence was achieved. As in Java, it had remained a somewhat alien factor in the independence movement. Aung San, the charismatic wartime leader and others of the Thakin group had adapted some ideas of Marxism-Leninism and rejected others. In Java, Sukarno and his colleagues from the *Partai Indonesia* had done the same. For the masses, whether reflective-passive or enormously vital, the new rigorous gospel from the West had even less appeal. From the messianic point of view it might have caused a short-lived interest, but its denial of the prospects of individual salvation created, for some time at least, an insurmountable barrier.

6. MASS RESPONSE IN VIETNAM

In 1911 Pham Phat Sanh, son of a policeman of Cholon, having practised sorcery for some years, had convinced himself that he had a claim to the Vietnamese throne. In order to procure the necessary funds he told two sorcerer colleagues to go and get an old tramp and to revere him as a living Buddha. Since people believed in such things, it would not be too difficult to find a sufficient number of followers who then could pay for the future plans. The tramp was found and he started his Buddahood in October 1911 in a small village. A few days later, when the village elders had found out what was going on, he was, together with his two companions, arrested and expelled. Shortly thereafter, the living Buddha died. People were now invited to revere his shrine in a bicycle-repair shop, where he could send messages from heaven. In March 1913, the message read that Pham Phat Sanh as Emperor Phan Xich Long would descend from heaven, to drive the French away and start his rule. When the day arrived six hundred Vietnamese, all clad in holiday clothes, came from the villages to the designated place to welcome the new emperor. The French police came too, dispersed the group and arrested the pretender.[23]

This story, though by no means typical of the Vietnamese response to French colonial rule, is, however, symptomatic of the people's religious beliefs. Bodhisattva speculations and what else was left of Buddhism could become a plaything in the hands of sorcerers. Those who were attracted to the movement in the case quoted did not come to improve their *karma* but to improve their material well-being. They were promised mandarin ranks in the future empire against cash in advance. A tramp could play the role of the Buddha and not even rouse suspicion. People obviously had curious ideas about the Lord. Even the bonzes, living in pagodas in the mountains, spoke about the Buddha as "a genius, gifted with supernatural powers", or as a "supreme being", who "is always present" and "who knows our impure thoughts", but who also "can heal us from sickness" by applying a "mysterious formula".[24]

These monks, who cared so little about the real teachings of the Buddha, did not preach peace, as did their colleagues in Upper Burma, but preached war after colonial rule had been instituted. They even supported their enemies of old, the mandarins, when the latter took up the leadership in the struggle against the French invaders. After "pacification" the bonzes were active in the secret societies. They finally saw their chance to gain some following among the people. One monk in 1914-16 created perfectly-organized resistance groups in thirteen out of twenty provinces in Cochin China.[25]

The Vietnamese, indeed, had not "learned their lesson", when the court at Hué officially surrendered. There was no *Sangha* preaching peace, nor was there a messianic tradition of any importance, implying that there was no need to fight. Fighting therefore continued openly on the part of the old military mandarin (known under his title of the De Tham) in northern Tongking, who was killed in an ambush in 1913; and

[23]G. Coulet, *Les sociétés secrètes en terre d'Annam* (C. Ardin, Saigon, 1926), pp. 17, 35-45.
[24]*Ibid.*, pp. 128, 131, 304.
[25]*Ibid.*, pp. 21, 157-65.

on the part of revolutionaries such as Phan Boi Chau and
Prince Cuong De, who had found asylum in Japan, and, after
1910, in South China. Through letters from abroad, by satirical
poems and by emissaries they encouraged the people to continue their opposition. And this opposition found its manifesta-
tion inside the country in all forms of secret society with the one
declared purpose of ousting the French.

Secret societies in Vietnam, of course, were older than the
French occupation. They were part and parcel of the Chinese
tradition. In the past they had been the ideal means by which
sorcerers like the emperor of our story could try to improve
their material well-being. Now they were also created for
seditious purposes, preparing bombs and planning insurrection.
Bombs were thrown in Vietnam as early as 1912 and the first
victim fell in 1913. It is worth looking more closely at these
secret societies, since they have not found proper attention in
the books dealing with the emancipation of Vietnam, though
there were at least two hundred of them by 1916.

Newcomers, whether they came voluntarily or had been
forced to come, were received in a solemn atmosphere. Some
blood was taken of all of those present, mixed with alcohol and
drunk after all had made a vow which went something like the
following:

> I pledge fraternal friendship to all of you. In good times
> as in adversity I shall share profits and misfortunes with
> my brothers. I shall get them out of trouble and I shall be
> united with them inseparably in life and death. I shall
> persevere until the end. May heaven and earth, the
> demons and the genii crush me right here if I lie.[26]

This was followed by a common meal and thereafter a written
form of the oath was burned on the shrine of the local genius.
Stressed again, was the determination to liberate the country,
to help each other in trouble, to obey the orders of the master,
to refrain from stealing and rape, to be conciliatory among
friends, to show pity for the poor and to be ready to die for the
just cause.

[26] *Ibid.*, pp. 104-05.

Such points as ousting the foreigners, punishing the traitors, helping one's neighbours and obeying orders appear again and again in the oaths of the various societies. What was most striking was the sometimes complete subordination to the leaders and their commands. Take for instance, the following oath taken in a secret society in early 1914:

> I pledge absolute loyalty to the four persons who receive this my vow. I shall never desert them, whatever the circumstances are. If I break this vow, my descendants, for three generations, may suffer from all sorts of evil.[27]

This reminds one of cadre discipline in a time when there was neither a Soviet Russia nor a Third International, six years before Ho Chi Minh heard of Lenin for the first time. When the Communists under Ho's leadership some ten years later tried to organize the masses, they did not have to apply principles, never heard of before: leadership, discipline, secrecy, terror if need be—it was all there, not dormant but vividly alive.

The perseverance of the Vietnamese in their opposition to French rule had two consequences: the French thought they could not dare to do what the British did in Rangoon and the Dutch did in Batavia, namely, to create a parliamentary stage, where government and colonial policy could be criticized openly. In the *Conseil Colonial* in Saigon criticism from the few Vietnamese, mainly from the careerist type, certainly was not encouraged by the *colons*, who were the great majority in the council. In the advisory councils in the protectorates of Annam and Tongking politics were not discussed at all. Even a party as moderate in its demands as was the Constitutionalist Party of Bui Quang Chieu met fierce opposition and was severely restricted in its activities. Therefore, leaders who wanted to articulate the grievances of the people were forced to go underground and resort to violence. Nguyen Thai Hoc, the leader of the *Viet-Nam-Quoc-Dan-Dang* shortly before his execution in May 1931 wrote a letter to the French parliament, in which he stated that he had subscribed to violent means of political

---

[27] *Ibid.*, p. 113.

action only after all attempts at legal activities had been rejected.[28]

The Communists, of course, with their Vietnamese Revolutionary Youth League (*Viet-Nam-Cach-Menh-Thanh-Nien-Chi-Hoi*, or *Thanh-Nien* for short) soon dominated the various revolutionary movements in Vietnam. Though there were some internal quarrels about the tactics to be applied, they, in general, worked rather successfully. Their rigorous application of disciplinary measures, and the readiness of the peasants to be organized, led to the creation of Soviets or *Xo-Viets*, as they were called, in Central Vietnam as early as 1930. Some of them in the Nghe-Tinh area were able to resist the drastic purge by the French in 1930-31 for almost a year.

The determination of the Vietnamese peasants to stand up for their rights stood in marked contrast to the Saya San Rebellion going on in Burma at the same time. In Burma, in the words of Maurice Collis,

> it was a magical rebellion. The old Burma which I have described, the Burma that dreamt of a saviour king, believed that a saviour king had come. For months there had been secret confabulations in jungle villages. The astrologers had given their verdict that at last the hour was at hand . . . The folklore of the whole East was on parade.[29]

In Vietnam, according to press accounts of the time,[30] the inhabitants of a village would gather, formulate resolutions and walk for miles to the next administrative post. Sometimes it

[28]L. Roubaud, *Vietnam: la tragedie indochinoise* (Librairie Valois, Paris, 1931), quotes the letter in full, see pp. 146-49.

[29]M. Collis, *Into Hidden Burma* (Faber and Faber, London, 1953), pp. 192, 194. A similar account by Collis on the Burmese rebellion is given in his *Trials in Burma* (Faber and Faber, London, 1938), pp. 208-15.

[30]See, for instance, *Le Temps* of 5 August 1930, "Lettre de Cochinchine: jours de révoltes", and *Le Temps* of 11 November 1930, "Lettre du Tonkin: les rebellions du Nord-Annam", which discuss the *manifestations* in detail. A good account of the course of revolutionary activities in Vietnam in the early 1930s is given in the eye-witness reports of L. Roubaud, *op. cit.*, and of A. Viollis, *Indochine S.O.S.* (Editeurs francais réunis, Paris, 1949; 1st pub. 1935).

was fifty, sometimes it was two hundred persons or a thousand who marched, not with the intention of the lieutenants of Saya San of killing the Europeans, but rather of presenting their demands. And those demands were, for instance, tax-reductions for the poor at the rate of one piastre per person, the introduction of an adequate taxation of the rich, the bringing in of a bill forbidding rice exports in times of famine, or the release of recently-captured prisoners.

This strong determination to stand up for one's rights, free from all irrational overtones, the discipline, the mutual reliance based on ancient communal bonds finally forced the French to leave the country. Vietnam was the only country under consideration which did not need messianic kings or foreign help either to mobilize or organize the people. The masses were ready to fight before the arrival of the Japanese and before the Communists took over the control of the movement. It was only that the latter could organize them on a broader scale.

CONCLUSION

Tradition, no doubt, has made itself felt in the emancipation of Southeast Asia from colonial rule. Its influence was to be found not so much among the majority of the leaders—they resembled each other closely in the three countries under study in their reactions, in their efforts and in their demands. Because of their education, their insight and their urge for modernization they turned away from traditional concepts and traditional values, some less, like the associationists, some more, like the constitutionalists and a good proportion of the revolutionaries. But, since the latter depended on the support of the masses, there was also a group which, for tactical reasons or uncon-sciously, upheld traditional values, not in order to return to the past but to reach the golden future by means of indigenous abilities and dispositions. These were the truly charismatic leaders, trying to lead their people out of the world of yesterday along familiar ways to a better tomorrow.

The masses could not be expected to respond to concepts totally alien to them. It is therefore no surprise that tradition has left its mark on modern Southeast Asia too. We have found a reflective passivity characteristic of Java, turbulent activity characteristic of Burma, disciplined determination characteristic of Vietnam. This was so at the beginning of colonial rule and this probably is still so today. It may be more surprising, however, to notice that the marked difference in the attitude towards Communism in Vietnam on the one hand, and Java and Burma on the other, has its roots in the respective traditions also. In Java and Burma, the Indianized countries, the prospects of individual salvation, messianism and further soteriological aspects in the respective religio-cultural traditions have proved, so far at least, to be an insurmountable barrier for Communism. In Sinicized Vietnam, as in China herself, there was no messianic tradition of any importance, there were no prospects of individual salvation and no preparations for the life hereafter. This would have meant a waste of energies which were needed in this life, and it was this life alone which counted. Thus the mandarins had done away with the soteriological aspects in the religio-cultural tradition and in doing this had done away with the barrier against Communism.

V

The Social Construction of
Tradition: an Interactionist View
of Social Change

JOSEPH R. GUSFIELD*

I

THE RECENT DISCUSSION of modernization theory by critics of functional and evolutionary concepts carries with it implications for the imagery and perspectives with which social scientists conceive of social change as a process. Recent criticisms have been directed at the use of concepts which utilize polar opposites, as beginning and end points in social and cultural change.[1] In conventional views of social change, the encounter between the colonial and colonizing people, between the West and the non-West and between the industrial and the peasant societies of the world is depicted as having brought about a series of conflicts and transitions from a static

---

* Professor of Sociology, University of California, San Diego.

[1]For some of these criticisms see Reinhard. Bendix, "Tradition and Modernity Reconsidered", *Comparative Studies in Society and History*, IX (1966-67), pp. 292-346 and my "Tradition and Modernity: Misplaced Polarities in the Study of Social Change", *American Journal of Sociology*, LXXII (January 1967), pp. 351-62. For a "rejoinder" see S. N. Eisenstadt, "Reflections on a Theory of Modernization" in Arnold Rifkin (ed.), *Nations by Design* (Doubleday, Anchor Books, New York, 1968), pp. 35-61.

society to a moving one. In this encounter, old and fixed traditions are assumed to be poorly adapted to new situations. Men must make choices between the old and the new. New forms replace the old or are successfully resisted.[2] In this formation what is "old" and traditional is assumed to be comparatively uniform, persistent and clear. What is past is clear and has only to be discovered, like pebbles on a beach.

More complex and sophisticated views of tradition are also found among social scientists. The work of Robert Redfield and of other students of India has replaced a homogeneous view of a single tradition with a perspective that stresses sharp differences between the literate and the popular; between the "great tradition" and the "little tradition".[3] Here processes of modernization, including literacy and increasing channels of communication, have operated to reinforce and spread the classic Hindu civilization of the urban literati through village, town and city.

Another significant departure from the view that "tradition" is unproblematically given is found in the description and analysis of cultural revivals. The study of national movements in Asia and Africa has given attention to the ways in which attacks on colonial domination have often been accompanied by movements to revive, extend and defend customs associated with less cosmopolitan and more "folk-like" sectors of the population.[4] Here, as in the concepts of great and little

[2]A major statement of this view is contained in the influential study by Daniel Lerner and Lucille Pevsner, *The Passing of Traditional Society* (The Free Press, Glencoe, Illinois, 1958).

[3]Robert Redfield, *Peasant Society* (University of Chicago Press, Phoenix Books, Chicago, 1960), ch. 3; Kim Marriott, "Little Communities in an Indigenous Civilization" in *idem* (ed.), *Village India* (Asia Publishing House, New Delhi, 1955).

[4]For descriptions of such phenomena in several national contexts see Charles Heimsath, *Indian Nationalism and Hindu Social Reform* (Princeton University Press, Princeton, 1964), chs 6, 12; Clifford Geertz, "The Integrative Revolution" in *idem* (ed.), *Old Societies and New States* (The Free Press, Glencoe, Illinois, 1963), pp. 105-58; Immanuel Wallerstein, *Africa: The Politics of Independence* (Vintage Books, New York, 1961), ch. 7; Rupert Emerson, *From Empire to Nation* (Harvard University Press, Cambridge, 1960), part 2.

tradition, the assumption is retained that these aspects of culture were once dominant but have now become dormant. The movement attempts to revive the dormant:

> Blyden urged Africans to emancipate themselves from the mental slavery imposed by European cultures and to *rediscover* themselves. (Italics mine, J. R. G.) He urged them to establish their own independent churches and a West African university where African studies would be welcomed and respected. [5]

Such views have formed the stock of structural anthropology and sociology. They have taken their basic units in the form of "cultures" and "societies" as given and have tended to see changes in culture or tradition as reflecting a transition from one state of being to another. The problems of achieving cultural identity, as in nationalist and independence movements, are thus viewed as problems of recovering or expressing existing or past cultures rather than as creation of new ones.

"Culture", however, is not alone a descriptive term, indicating to the observer the unique content of a group's way of life. It also has a reflexive dimension. The actor can perceive of himself and his behaviour as cultural, as signifying the unique character of his group, community or "sub-culture". It is as an aspect of a present situation that a group shares a definition of itself as possessing a culture or a tradition with a particular content. Conceptions of past and future, of tradition and modernity, of culture itself are all phenomena about which people can think and toward which they can be self-conscious.

This reflexive character of tradition is the inciting point for the present paper. In analysing "traditional culture" as an idea we will describe and analyse movements which have played significant roles in identifying the uniqueness of social groups and the content of their own culture. The materials will be drawn mostly from Japan, India and the United States. In treating movements for self-identification and cultural change

[5] J. F. Ayai, "The Place of African History and Culture in the Process of Nation-Building in Africa South of the Sahara" in I. Wallerstein (ed.), *Social Change: The Colonial Situation* (John Wiley, New York, 1966), pp. 606-16, at p. 608.

as reflexive, we emphasize that these are movements of both self-discovery and of self-definition and redefinition. Rather than solely discovered, tradition is also created and constructed out of alternative forms. As Kim Marriott has put it ". . . the 'national' culture of every new state is a product of modern manufacture".[6] It is more than that, however; it is also a belief and a statement about what is *now* perceived as having been typical in the *past*.

Monographs on primitive societies seldom contain material about such reflexive concerns as we find in peasant and industrial societies. They do not reveal a folk anthropology showing that the members of the tribe are self-conscious of their culture. Herodotus distinguished between "Greeks" and "barbarians", but this is a long way from the quest for identity which marks the phenomena of national, regional, and other communal movements. This suggests that consciousness of culture, as defining the uniqueness of a group or people, is itself a product of particular experiences. Ethnic identity is enhanced in the interaction between peoples, even those previously unaware of themselves as similar. In his study of the Chinese in Hawaii, Glick points out that the migrants from the Cantonese area, from the Peking area, from northern, central and southern China did not perceive of themselves as at all part of a common people or culture until they found this to be the case in the eyes of the residents of Hawaii.[7]

One would need to search in a history not yet written for the development of the reflexive idea of culture. Kroeber and Kluckhohn found the origins of the term "culture" in the universal histories of German philosophers and historians appearing toward the end of the eighteenth century.[8] But there

[6]Kim Marriott, "Cultural Policy in the New States" in C. Geertz (ed.), *op. cit.*, pp. 27-57 at p. 56. For a general discussion of ethnic consciousness as it develops in interaction with other groups see Tamotsu Shibutani and Kian M. Kwan, *Ethnic Stratification* (Macmillan, New York, 1965), ch. 2.

[7]Clarence Glick, "The Relation Between Position and Status in the Assimilation of Chinese in Hawaii", *American Journal of Sociology*, XLVII (1942), pp. 667-79.

[8]A. L. Kroeber and Clyde Kluckhohn, *Culture* (Vintage Books, New York, 1952), part I.

its usage remains fairly close to the concept of "civilization" rather than "culture" as we use it here. It also suggests that as a term "culture" appears earlier and more popularly in Germany as a synonym for "society" than it does in France or England. Kroeber and Kluckhohn interpret this as a result of greater differentiation between areas in the pre-national German area than in the other two countries. This interpretation is for them also enhanced by what they feel to be the greater popularity of the term in the United States than in the more culturally homogeneous societies of France and England.[9]

In his analysis of nineteenth-century English literature the critic Raymond Williams finds the concept of culture emergent with the advent of industrialization and the growing separation of classes.[10] The working-class conception of a "working-class culture" required specific conditions of class differentiation. Culture in the conventional anthropologist's sense of a "localized more or less different and unique system of behaviour, e.g. Eskimo culture, Cherokee Indian culture" is itself problematic. It would take the much-needed work of a good cultural historian to do for the idea and consciousness of culture what recently some of the British historians of industrialization or of the French Revolution have attempted to do for concepts of "class".[11]

In this paper we are not concerned with how traditions change but rather with how a given content is itself defined as traditional. How it is that groups designate themselves and define the content of their histories and characteristics? How do such definitions change? How is the "traditional" itself constructed?

In analysing the uses of tradition, we are investigating how and why groups define events, structures or values as being part of the past. To confer this meaning of "pastness" is not a neutral matter. For many it gives a special legitimacy to that which is defined as traditional or derived from it. The

[9]*Ibid.*, p. 68.

[10]Raymond Williams, *Culture and Society: 1780-1950* (Anchor Books, New York, 1959).

[11]Alfred Cobban, *The Social Interpretation of the French Revolution* (Cambridge University Press, Cambridge, 1964).

past has a sacred aura about it and in the publicly defined conflicts between the traditional and the modern it often matters very much what a particular set of ideas can be labelled.[12]

II

We begin with Japanese society. The success story of Japanese industrialization is too well-known to be recounted again here. For our purposes what is so intriguing is the impact of that story on conceptions of social change which social scientists had held in the past. Japan has appeared as a contradiction to the theories of the linear evolution of Western societies from feudalism to capitalism, from tradition to modernity and from folk to urban societies. The Japanese have presented us with a seeming amalgam of the feudal and the capitalist in which communal identities and loyalties reinforced and supported new modes of economic and technological activity.[13]

In the process of change, Japanese intellectuals and academics have themselves been engaged in characterizing Japanese culture. John Bennett has recently pointed out that Japanese scholars, as well as foreign scholars, have wavered in their characterizations. At several times the communal characteristics of a high level of solidarity and a functioning hierarchy were seen as continuing to be characteristic of the Japanese. At other times they were viewed as disappearing with Western influences.[14] Consensus has shifted back and forth. The Japanese have been concerned with modernization and tradition, sometimes seeing in the latter a barrier to the former

[12]See the general analyses of tradition in Edward Shils, "Tradition", *Comparative Studies in Society and History*, XIII (April 1971), pp. 122-59, esp. pp. 138-44.

[13]For some accounts of this process see Josefa Saniel, "The Mobilization of Traditional Values in the Modernization of Japan" in Robert Bellah (ed.), *Religion and Progress in Modern Asia* (The Free Press, New York, 1965), pp. 124-50, and Thomas C. Smith, "Japan's Aristocratic Revolution", *Yale Review*, V (1960-1961), pp. 370-83.

[14]John Bennett, "Tradition, Modernity and Communalism in Japan's Modernization", *Journal of Social Issues*, XXIV (October 1968), pp. 25-44.

and sometimes stressing the detrimental effects of modernization in displacing traditional Japanese ways. Whatever the
ideology, there has often been an agreement that Japanese
culture has had a traditional set of customs and ways of be-
having which can be specified and which constitute that which
is changing or which resists further change.

What is now clear is that conceptions of the communal
character of Japan have themselves been responses to immediate situations. In this sense they have been part of the
process by which Japanese, operating through intellectualized
versions of culture, have created their culture in the process of
perceiving it. At each stage the observers and analysts have
defined the traditional past for that point in historical time.

An interesting form of such concerns can be seen in what is
often hailed as a typical illustration of traditional Japanese
communalism, the *nenkō* system—the pattern of lifetime
employment and of a wage structure geared to age and
seniority rather than productivity. The *nenkō* system was
brought to attention in American scholarship with the publication of James Abegglen's book *The Japanese Factory*.[15] In his
description of the system, Abegglen described a dual pattern of
loyalty of the worker to the firm and of the firm to the worker.
Here again was another illustration of the way in which a
feudal culture not only continued to exist in capitalist Japan
but even became the basis for industrial relations in the citadel
of Westernized technology and economics—large-scale manu-
facturing. On the basis of this Abegglen insisted that economic
mobility was non-existent in Japan; that the market of classical
economics was sharply limited by the continuation of Japanese
traditions of communalism.

The view of the *nenkō* system as a continuation of Japanese
labour relations on a feudal basis is among many myths of
cultural traditions. A closer look indicates that this unique
system of industrial relations developed in relationship to
intensive problems of labour turnover in the twentieth century.
Rather than being a continuation of an old tradition the

[15]James Abegglen, *The Japanese Factory* (The Free Press, Glencoe,
Illinois, 1958).

nenkō system is itself relatively recent and its origins go back not
much further than the 1920s.[16] Even today it is far less characteristic of the smaller establishments where communal ties
might seem to be most persistent. The idea that labour mobility
has been or is non-existent in Japan is also quite erroneous.
Both present and previous generations displayed relatively high
rates of job change.[17]

Significant in this history of ideas about Japanese mobility is
the extent to which recent change so quickly becomes viewed
as tradition.[18] Abegglen's view has not seemed to the Japanese
critics of it simply an anomaly of Western ignorance. It has
also been a view utilized by Japanese scholars until recently.[19]
It has taken considerable pains of research to develop alternate
findings which altered the view of Japanese "tradition" and
showed its complexity.

We are not trying to prejudge the issue of the relationship
between Japanese communalism and the *nenkō* system by
pointing to its recency but merely to indicate that tradition has
a phenomenological characteristic. People define their cultures
and their traditions. They are not necessarily metaphysical
entities given in the nature of things; they are not Durkheimian
"social facts" but are instead cut and ordered and chosen,

[16]For discussion of the sources of *nenkō*, see Koji Taira, "The Characteristics of Japanese Labor Markets", *Economic Development and Cultural
Change*, X, 1 (January 1962), pp. 150-68; Solomon Levine, "Labor Relations in Japan" in William Lockwood (ed.), *State and Economic Development in
Japan* (Princeton University Press, Princeton, 1965). For a recent field study
see Robert Cole, *Japanese Blue Collar* (University of California Press,
Berkeley, 1971).

[17]Ken'ichi Tominaga, "Occupation Mobility in Japanese Society",
The Journal of Economic Behaviour, II (April 1962), pp. 1-37; Taira, *op. cit.*
The findings concerning small and large establishments in Japan are based
on an unpublished study by Gusfield and Tominaga.

[18]This is by no means confined to Japan. For other examples see my
"Tradition and Modernity", *op. cit.* For an American example which docu-
ments the relative "recency" of a "tradition" see C. Vann Woodward,
The Strange Career of Jim Crow (Oxford University Press, New York, 1955).

[19]Y. Scott Matsumoto, *Contemporary Japan* (*Transactions of the American
Philosophical Society*, new series, L, part 1; Philadelphia, American Philo-
sophical Society, 1960); Chie Nakane, *Japanese Society* (University of
California Press, Berkeley, 1970); Cole, *op. cit.*, esp. pp. 7-11.

products of a social process. Whether or not earlier "feudal" Japanese institutions, such as the *oyabun-kobun* (patron-worker) relationship, were precursors of the *nenko* system is a matter debated by scholars.[20] What is evident, however, is that the "real" situation is itself ambiguous and that self-definitions of "traditional" Japanese communalism using the *nenko* system are constructions of that tradition rather than continuances, rediscoveries or revivals.

Still another instance from the Japanese case will show us how ambiguities involved in understanding the past can be resolved and "traditional culture" determined and defined as a political act. Here the example is drawn from the Meiji Restoration and the characteristic loyalty to the emperor, which so many foreigners have seen as deeply embedded in Japanese traditional conceptions of the relation between the self and the state.

In a fascinating bit of exposition, the author of a textbook on Japanese politics introduces a chapter on "The Emperor: the Nation's Symbol and Rallying Point" by saying, "The emperor has been and still is the living symbol of the nation's history, heritage, and achievements, of all that is glorious in the nation's past and present, of its continuity and durability".[21] In a footnote to the paragraph he writes, however, ". . . this has not always been so for it is a relatively recent development which accompanied Japan's emergence as a modern power in the nineteenth century".[22] The scholar giveth and the scholar taketh away.

Belief in the dominant role of the emperor in the Japanese state has seemed a traditional part of Japan continued into its modern phase and therefore a great source of continuity with feudal Japan. Nevertheless, it is the case that both Japanese and Western students of Japanese history recognize that the actual status of the emperor in pre-Meiji Japan has often been incon-

---

[20]See the differences between the Taira and Levine papers cited above and the view of John Bennett and Iwo Ishino, *Paternalism in the Japanese Economy* (University of Minnesota Press, Minneapolis, 1963).

[21]Chitoshi Yanaga, *Japanese People and Politics* (John Wiley, New York, 1956), p. 129.

[22]*Idem.*, note 1.

sistent with the position given to him by the Meiji constitution.[23] The position of the emperor *vis-à-vis* the government and the people of Japan has fluctuated through its
history. No matter how one interprets the varying status of the
emperor, what is implied by the phrase "the Meiji Restoration"
involves but a decided break with what had existed through the
Tokugawa period and not a continuity with tradition. In this
sense the present form of loyalty of the individual citizen to the
emperor and the importance of the emperor in the state system
dates from 1868. Giving it the status of the traditional heightens
its legitimacy.

The philosophy which gave the emperor so central a role in
the life of the citizen and the state as implied by the Imperial
Rescript of 1890 on education was not a reiteration of a clearly-
defined culture. It was instead the almost deliberate development by an élite of a myth of loyalty as part of past cultural
tradition. It served to provide a cohesion and consensus which
was stressed in the effort to centralize and nationalize Japan.
"The state improved the material condition of the court and
invested it with new glamour and aura. Criticism of the throne
was silenced and a system went into effect which made it
difficult, if not impossible, for there to be open disagreements
between the Imperial Court and the government".[24] The
Meiji élite thus became the definers of the tradition and its
change. In "restoring" the emperor they were defining a pre-
Tokugawa Japan whose characteristics of imperial power are
by no means clear. In this fashion Japanese culture was not only
being found or revived; it was being formed.

The Japanese situation has provided us with two examples
of the ambiguity in the concept of a traditional culture. What
appeared to have been continuations of phenomena existing for

---

[23]Herschel Webb, "The Development of an Orthodox Attitude Toward
the Imperial Institution in the Nineteenth Century" in Marius Jansen (ed.),
Changing Japanese Attitudes Toward Modernization (Princeton University
Press, Princeton, 1965), pp. 167-92.

[24]*Ibid.*, pp. 184-85. For the importance of the emperor in establishing
Japanese identity during modernization see Kenneth Pyle, *The New
Generation in Meiji Japan* (Stanford University Press, Stanford, 1969),
pp. 94-96, 124-26.

centuries—the *nenkō* system of industrial relations and the dominance of the emperor in the Japanese system—are *not* unambiguously "traditional". In both cases the designation of these behaviour patterns as an ongoing part of continuing Japanese culture was constructed. The latter case, that of the emperor, is illustrative of the role that political authority can play in determining and defining the group culture.

III

Unlike Japan, India represents a society of immense diversities where region, caste and religion all constitute important sources for primordial identification. The question is often asked: Is India a nation? The development of the nationalist movement stirred into being an all-India identification, but the process of increasing communications and political hegemony has also accentuated regional unities. In the development of national and sub-national groupings Indian social structure today presents a remarkable process of group formation and self-designation through cultural revival. In Africa Westernized intellectuals accentuated supposed African styles of life into a philosophy of "negritude". Similarly the Indian nationalist movement produced efforts to reinstate the styles of life and forms of culture identified with the non-Western and the traditional in India.

This process, which Georges Balandier calls "rehabilitation of culture",[25] is by no means simply a reaching out and grabbing of a well-defined conception and then putting it on like an old overcoat. In the process the tradition itself is as much formed as it is discovered. The nationalist movement gave considerable impetus to an all-India culture. It stressed those symbols of "great tradition" which could be accepted at popular levels. Since Independence the quest for symbols of India, as distinct from that of specific sub-communities, has made it necessary to

---

[25]Georges Balandier, "Political Myths of Colonization and Decolonization in Africa" (trans. by Jean-Guy Vaillancourt) in Reinhard Bendix *et al.* (eds), *State and Society* (Little, Brown, New York, 1968), pp. 475-84 at p. 479.

expand and reinforce symbols and legends which have been little used in the past. Kim Marriott has shown how Aśoka and the symbol of the lions, little-known aspects of the Indian past, were "rescued" from history because they represented Indian symbols which, in a period of communal conflict, would not be offensive to any group.[26] Thus the traditional culture is itself defined by new myths of the past. In similar fashion, Milton Singer has shown how the role of the brahmin in the Bhakti movements in contemporary Madras involves a reformulation of classic, Sanskritized elements into new modes of cultural performance and into new forms such as movies and music.[27] Sanskritization therefore involves more than imitation. It also involves an imputation or judgement about the content of that tradition. What is perceived as Sanskritic and ancient may actually be new mint.

Those forces which act to expand the arena of political and economic association in India deeply affect the construction of tradition. They provide the conditions, the occasions and the rewards for elaborating a consciousness of group membership and identity. One result of electoral politics and independence has been the intensification of movements for change in caste position. Frequently these involve new cultural content now defined as being old and pre-existing patterns. In this smelting process new group identities are forged.

These demands for reformulation must be seen in the context of Indian caste competition and conflict intensified by the political process of electoral democracy. The political importance of numbers and the economic concerns emergent on regional and national bases make for the development of new associations in which caste and other communal identities are sources for new groupings. The rise of caste associations appears to be an important part of a tendency for Indian society

[26]Kim Marriott, "Cultural Policy in the New States" in Geertz (ed.), *op. cit.*, pp. 35-36.

[27]Milton Singer, "The Radha Krishna *Bhajanas* of Madras City" in *idem* (ed.), *Krishna: Myths, Rites and Attitudes* (Chicago University Press, Phoenix Books, Chicago, 1968), pp. 90-139; also "The Great Tradition of Hinduism in the City of Madras" in Charles Leslie (ed.), *Anthropology of Folk Religion* (Vintage Books, New York, 1960), pp. 105-68.

to develop new and extra-local groups.[28] Castes are also now formed by uniting local "castes" in wider ones. These emerge when common interests, cultural similarities and similar general caste category make it possible for local groups to pull together with groups from other localities to pursue aims and goals which exist at the state and national levels. In this process the caste uses whatever is available in the "culture" and develops the presupposition of its own common culture.[29] It proceeds to act "as if" the status now sought is the reality of old.

In one common pattern of mobility, the classic form of Indian social change is used and heightened. Here the caste proceeds to take on styles of life associated with brahmins.[30] Such Sanskritization involves the redefinition of tradition through leadership. The caste panchayat has provided a model of central control which has made it possible to state and reinforce demands for greater Sanskritizing of the caste culture. In this fashion whole styles of life shifts can and have been developed quickly. These have involved changes in such culture contents as eating habits, clothing style and marriage customs. This has been described in a number of cases when previously lower

[28]The rise of caste associations and consequent shifting character of caste as a unit of social structure is a dominant theme in the sociology of post-Independence India. From a large literature of empirical studies and analysis the following are among leading statements: M. N. Srinivas, *Social Change in Modern India* (University of California Press, Berkeley, 1966); Lloyd I. Rudolph and Susanne Hoeber Rudolph, *The Modernity of Tradition: Political Development in India* (University of Chicago Press, Chicago, 1967), Part 1; André Béteille, "Elites, Status Groups, and Caste in Modern India" in Philip Mason (ed.), *India and Ceylon: Unity and Diversity* (Oxford University Press, London, 1967), pp. 223-43; articles by M. N. Srinivas, William Rowe and Owen Lynch in M. Singer and B. S. Cohn (eds), *Structure and Change in Indian Society* (Aldine, Chicago, 1968), pp. 189-242.

[29]See the case of the Shanans who became Nadars and the Pallis who became Vanniyars and the legitimation of their mobility through political exchange in Rudolph & Rudolph, *op. cit.*, pp. 36-64.

[30]The concept of Sanskritization has been developed in describing and explaining this process. The seminal statement is M. N. Srinivas, "A Note on Sanskritization and Westernization" reprinted in his *Caste in Modern India* (Asia Publishing House, New Delhi, 1962), pp. 42-62.

castes have used their political power to enable them to "make good" their claims to new styles and thus legitimate their new positions.[31]

In these cases, the quest for social mobility has frequently carried with it "rediscovery of the past". The new status is bolstered by efforts to prove that myths that reinforced a lower position in the society are false; that in truth the history of the caste has not been recognized correctly in the past. Having developed new aspirations and often new economic capabilities, members of the caste find it essential for their own personal mobility that the mobility of the caste also be raised. The new mythologies are therefore the development of wholly new "traditions" by which the caste or regional group seeks its new level and expresses its new self-confidence.[32]

The movement for a traditional identity also exists where new groups come into being. The impact of a common Westernized style of life and associations has cut across previously exclusive castes and sub-castes. Common life styles are generating the development of totally new groups, especially among Indian élites. These define themselves as new sub-castes in a similar process to that which we have just described above for pre-existent ones. As André Béteille has shown, the development of mythology and tradition helps to cloak the changes which are occurring and which would be very difficult to define

---

[31]In addition to the work of M. N. Srinivas and the Rudolphs cited above see also Robert L. Hardgrave, Jr, *The Nadars of Tamilnad: Culture of a Community in Change* (University of California Press, Berkeley, 1969); Owen Lynch, *The Politics of Untouchability* (Columbia University Press, New York, 1969); André Béteille, *Caste, Class and Power* (University of California Press, Berkeley, 1965). For a general account of these mobility processes, with many examples of castes, see David Mandelbaum, *Society in India*, vol. II (University of California Press, Berkeley, 1970), chs 23-27.

[32]See the account of caste mythologies in Hardgrave, *op. cit.*, ch. 3, and in Lynch, *op. cit.*, ch. 4. The process is similar to that found in Edmund Leach, *Political Systems of Highland Burma* (Bell, London, 1964), ch. 9, "Myth as a Justification for Faction and Social Change". Irschick finds the same process in the use of the myth of Dravidian origin. See Eugene Irschick, *Politics and Social Conflict in South India: The Non-Brahman Movement and Tamil Separatism, 1916-1929* (University of California Press, Berkeley, 1969), p. 278 *ff.* & p. 354 *ff.*

in older terms.[33]

It is not that caste as a system of human relationships is either disappearing or continuing in India that is significant for our argument. What we are stressing is that the caste idiom and the normative structure of caste loyalty and interest are used as a part of the available materials out of which to fashion new mechanisms of group formation and action. In its use structures and "cultures" come into being which are legitimated as if they were part of an existing culture.

The conventionally understood forms of cultural identity of course also go on. Here the group reinforces and re-establishes what they have been doing in the past. Now, however, they are self-conscious about it. The conflicts and opportunities attendant in the political process and in the contact between a variety of local groups make it necessary to define and defend styles of life and group memberships as bases for political trust and obligation. How deeply the process of identity is also the process of new identity is revealed in the extensiveness to which castes undergo changes in name as well as changes in behaviour. A saying among Indian Muslims expresses the process: "Last year we were weavers, this year we are Shaikhs and next year if the harvest is good we shall be Sayyids".[34]

One of the clearest examples of the process of culture change as culture invention can be seen in the development of linguistic movements in India and in their impact on language, especially in the period since Independence. There is no element of culture seemingly as deeply part of a people as its language. Yet this too involves both the process of self-designation of a language as "ours" and the similar process of reinforcement or rejection of prevalent or suggested linguistic habits and styles. Once again our reference is not to the general sense in which language changes under shifting conditions such as migration and education. We are rather calling attention here

[33]Béteille, "Elites, Status Groups and Caste in Modern India" in Mason (ed.), *op. cit.* See also T. Bottomore, "Cohesion and Division in Indian Elites" in *ibid.*, and M. N. Srinivas, "Mobility in the Caste System" in Singer and Cohn (eds), *op. cit.*

[34]Mandelbaum, *op. cit.*, p. 434. See also Rudolph & Rudolph, *op. cit.*, and Lynch, *op. cit.*

to those aspects which are political in that they involve mobilizations of people in explicit fashions and in conflict with others concerning control and use of state power.[35] What does a group perceive as "its" language? What aspects of its language are reinforced and rejected by considerations of identity? How do these rejections and acceptances affect the existing state of the language?

In the development of the Indian nationalist movement and in the Independence period, English has often seemed a paradoxical anomaly. In rejecting the colonizer the nationalist's use of the English language presented a problem, especially in the quest for an all-India and non-British style of life. Even those who favour the retention of English as an official language in India and reject the uses of Hindi have recognized the inconsistent position in which this places the Indian nationalist.

It is in this context that the move toward the development of the Hindi language has itself to be seen.[36] Linguists may argue about whether or not there "is" such a language as Hindi, given the diversities in dialect that exist across north India and the so-called Hindi plains. Certainly the language of areas which had been under the domination of the Muslims or which contained large Muslim populations included far more Urdu than did the non-Muslim sections of North India. Arguments over the content of the North Indian language were destined to reflect the political, cultural and religious conflicts that have divided groups in North India.

As national and regional and religious conflicts were sharpened, differentiation occurred precisely along these lines. A greater importation of Sanskrit occurred into Hinduized areas and a greater retention of Urdu in more Islamic sections.

---

[35]For a clear statement embodying this conventional approach see A. Taboret-Keller, "Sociological Factors of Language Maintenance and Language Shift" in Joshua A. Fishman, Charles A. Ferguson and Jyotirindra Das Gupta (eds), *Language Problems of Developing Nations* (John Wiley, New York, 1968).

[36]For an analysis of language policy and its development in India see Jyotirindra Das Gupta, *Language Conflict and National Development: Group Politics and National Language Policy in India* (University of California Press, Berkeley, 1970).

Words fell into disfavour because they came to be associated with one or another group. Gandhi, recognizing the implications of this for conflict, championed Hindustani, a less-Sanskritized version of a language which he felt would be mutually acceptable to the Hindus and Muslims.[37]

The development of Hindi imperialism would be far more difficult were the various states on the Gangetic plain to attempt to retain their specific languages as official public ones. An example of this is seen in the fear among the inhabitants of North Bihar that their regional importance within the state will be diminished by the usage of Hindi rather than their own Maithili. Here the argument about whether Maithili is a separate language or only a dialect of Hindi is more than just the linguist's scholarly problem.[38] The movement for retention of Maithili and its identification as a language distinct from Hindi has roots in political realities as well as regional pride.

The accompanying cultural revival, the discovery of the importance of older texts, and the quest for translating and publishing materials in the now-reinforced language supplies the facilities and impetus for fulfilling the prophecy that the language is indeed a common one and is essential to enable a given group to practise its culture. The political reinforcement of this through requirements for jobs and through the school system in turn now make the culture, in a sense of existing practices, square with the view by which it has been justified. Paul Brass has summed this up very well in referring to regional and national movements in India by saying:

> It appears, in fact, that such movements benefit more from the full freedom to select the desired symbols from the past than from the living embodiment of an historical-political tradition in the present.[39]

Both political and "cultural" leadership are responsible for a new language content. The Indian government has subsidized

[37]*Ibid.*, chs 4 and 5.
[38]Paul Brass, The Politics of Language: The Maithili Movement in North Bihar (Unpublished manuscript).
[39]*Ibid.*, p. 10.

the publication of Hindi materials, its use in broadcasting and translations of scientific and other materials from foreign languages into Hindi. New encyclopædias and dictionaries and the development of literary prizes have produced a seeming renaissance of Hindi in both written and verbal forms.[40]

This "renaissance" is deceptive. Much of the leadership in the work of disseminating Hindi has come from the literati of writers, artists and humanistic academics. These are introducing a "pure" or highly Sanskritized Hindi which is not a reflection of common elements in the Hindi used in the past in Northern India. The use of these forms of Hindi has been defended as efforts to produce a more standardized language, capable of being used in a wide area across local variations. Introduction of this "pure" Hindi on All-India Radio was met by protest of non-understandability.[41] Whatever the merit of the argument, the Hindi urged and institutionally supported as Indian neither represents the "great tradition" nor a folk culture:

> The guiding norm of going back to "Mother Sanskrit" and the unremitting zeal in purifying Hindi from all "alien" influences have created a language which may satisfy the regional pride of the Hindi leaders, but . . . the artificial product has tended to erect barriers between literary communication and mass communication.[42]

Such movements to define the culture of a given group succeed also in developing the groups. Language, by being now connected with a set of political and social loyalties and facilities, is now a source of group definition. The Hindi-speaking North is now a linguistic and political area. So too other groups, such as the Punjabi-speakers or the Dravidians, are mobilized in self-defence. The hauteur with which the Bengali talks about Hindi as an "upstart language" testifies to the ways in which tradition is invented as much as it is dis-

[40]Das Gupta, *op. cit.*, ch. 6.
[41]*Ibid.*, pp. 176-77.
[42]*Ibid.*, pp. 187-88.

covered and to the political importance which the process possesses.

The material from India is further illustration of socially-constructed traditions. It reinforces the analysis drawn from Japan. It adds to it, however, an understanding of the role such constructions play in the context of group diversities and political conflict. In modern India, new castes, communal groups and linguistic associations are formed through amalgams, alliances and revisions of old ones. National and regional consciousness are emergent new phenomena. "Tradition" and "culture" are constructed in the process of defining the group to itself through associations, intellectual products, political leadership and governmental sponsorship.

Conceptualizing such change as transitional points between "traditional" and "modern" society begs the question. First, the points of cultural emphasis around which loyalties of tradition congeal are often, as we have seen, products of present or recent occurrence. They are often constricted in a context of political conflict and/or government policy. Seeing them as vestiges of a past both falsifies the content and obscures the process. Secondly, the cultural revival and the renaissance of tradition are not only found in the nationalism and regionalism of new nations. They are also discoverable within old nations and affluent societies. Ethnic communalism does not disappear and its assertion can and does occur even generations after migration and "assimilation". Recent developments in the United States will illustrate this.

IV

That such movements can and do occur in highly-industrialized societies is seen in the movement connected with cultural identity among black people in the United States. The developing movement towards a greater political separation of the black community from the white is part of the present ideology of one wing of the Negro movement. It is not new. From time to time it has appeared in the general history of the movement, especially among the Garveyites in the 1920s and of course with the growth of the Black Muslim movement in the 1950s and 1960s.[43] Whatever may be the ultimate fate of the political ideology of black nationalism, certainly the development of black culture as part of the process of new identification of who "we are" and what are the unique aspects of being black is at present a very salient part of the movement in most black communities and in many political wings. Cultural nationalism has had an appreciative response.

So many scholars and intellectuals have commented on the problems of self-confidence and identity among the American Negro that it is by now an aspect of popular as well as literary perceptions.[44] Here the need to re-formulate the past is connected not only with political reasons for maintaining separateness but as a means of developing a sense of self-confidence. It is both intrinsically meritorious and essential as well for a movement that is in conflict with other aspects of the society.

The demand for courses and programmes of study at secondary and higher educational levels in areas of ethnic or black studies is again the concept of "re-establishing" traditions; here it is that of "rediscovering" Afro-American roots and revising the errors of past "white history". It is coupled also with a strong assertion that the Negro was robbed of his culture by slavery and by his treatment during the slave period. Thus new history is being written, as revisionist history frequently is.[45] As we have seen in Japan and in India, it is an open question as to whether past "false" history is now corrected or whether history, as often happens, is being revised

[43]For a historical survey of black nationalist movements in the United States see the introduction and materials in John Bracey, Jr, August Meier and Elliott Rudwick (eds), *Black Nationalism in America* (Bobbs-Merrill, Indianapolis, 1970).

[44]Erik H. Erikson, "The Concept of Identity in Race Relations" in T. Parsons and K. Clark (eds), *The Negro American* (Houghton-Mifflin, Boston, 1967) and Harold Isaacs, "Group Identity and Political Change: The Role of History and Origins." (Paper presented at the American Association for Asian Studies, San Francisco, 3 April 1965.)

[45]See John Higham (ed.), *The Reconstruction of American History* (Harper Torchbooks, New York, 1962); V. Monteil, "The Colonization of the Writing of History," in I. Wallerstein (ed.), *op. cit.*, pp. 585-91.

or reformulated in accordance with new needs for identity.[46] The question of the "truth" of history is separate from its import as myth and justification.

The rediscovery also takes the form of importation into present styles of living of Africanisms and of other styles associated with "the black folk". Thus the growing use of African dress, of "soul food", the extolling of the jazz and blues music and the shifting perception of Negro dialect as "mother tongue" is part of the impact of the movement on styles of living. Middle-class Negro families now find there are internal as well as external pressures to adopt the modes of living which may be strange to them but which are set forth as the culture that has been lost. This "going home" is now defined as "being natural".

Even the very name is part of this process. Thus the Negro has gone through a variety of different names by which he has designated himself to himself.[47] For much of the last half of the nineteenth century the term "colored people" was the dominant term and the development in 1905 of the National Association for the Advancement of Colored People is indicative of its wide acceptance. A number of leaders during the first half of the twentieth century made strong efforts to get rid of this as the term of self-designation. Thus Garvey called his secessionist group the Universal Negro Improvement Association. At present the term Negro has become associated with an earlier stage in history and the terms black or Afro-American are now more widely used. The use of the word "black" is itself enormously revealing of a strong effort to transvalue aspects associated heretofore with derogatory white designations and thus to change a negative self-conception into a positive one. Here again the theme of cultural nationalism implies an identity with "folk" themes and low-status sectors of the population.

[46]In addition to Monteil in Wallerstein (ed.), *op. cit.*, see the criticism of revisionist black history in Eugene Genovese, "The Roots of Black Nationalism" in Peter Rose (ed.), *Old Memories, New Moods* (Atherton Press, New York, 1970), pp. 31-52.

[47]Lerone Bennett, Jr, "What's in a Name?" in Rose (ed.), *op. cit.*, pp. 373-84.

In his defence of the use of the concept of black culture Robert Blauner has in many ways summarized this paper. Referring to criticisms of the use of black culture as either describing what does not exist or as describing a general American or southern lower-class culture, Blauner suggests that these are

> . . . based on a static, deterministic approach to cultural development, an approach which minimizes its open-ended quality and therefore underplays the role of consciousness and culture-building in effecting that development.[48]

The conventional approach to social change in many parts of the world has similarly been at fault in its static model of human behaviour. In viewing people as possessing fixed cultures that come into conflict with new situations, it ignores the reflexive character of human behaviours, it redefines culture and tradition as social facts that are more stubborn than our materials and perspectives would indicate.

The difficulty with this model is that it ignores both the ways in which new structures, new values and new self-perceptions emerge without clear-cut affiliation to either end of the polar opposites of tradition and modernity. The processes of social change involve interpretation and interaction between persons and situations that are both more complex and less fixed than that.

[48]Robert Blauner, "Black Culture: Myth or Reality?" in N. Whitten, Jr and John Szwed, *Afro-American Anthropology* (The Free Press, New York, 1970), pp. 347-75 at p. 349.